SO-AZH-948

TEN YEARS OF DISCOVERY
IN THE WILDERNESS OF JUDAEA

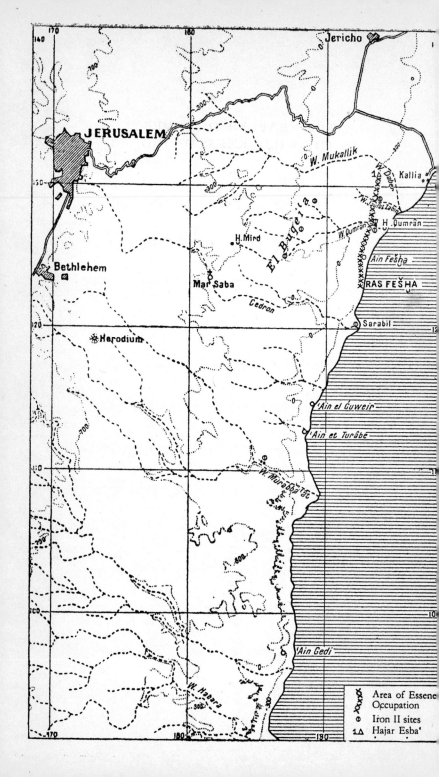

STUDIES IN BIBLICAL THEOLOGY

TEN YEARS OF DISCOVERY IN THE WILDERNESS OF JUDAEA

J. T. MILIK

Translated by
J. STRUGNELL

ALEC R. ALLENSON, INC
635 EAST OGDEN AVENUE
NAPERVILLE, ILL

Translated from the French
Dix ans de Découvertes dans le Désert de Juda
(Les Éditions du Cerf, Paris, 1957)

First English edition 1959
© SCM PRESS LTD 1959

NIHIL OBSTAT:
Hierosolymis, 10 iii 1958

JOSEPH A. FITZMYER, S.J.
Censor Delegatus

IMPRIMATUR:
Hierosolymis, 18 iii 1958

+ALBERTUS GORI, O.F.M.
Patriarcha

CONTENTS

Contents

PREFACE

The present work is a considerably revised and expanded translation of the French edition published by Les Editions du Cerf in 1957. Although the result is slightly more technical than was the French original, my intention is still to give a popular treatment of the subject, and for this reason I have only occasionally given references to the learned articles whose conclusions I have used. The non-academic reader should be warned that some of his fellows have found Chapter II rough going, and recommend, to my horror, that it can be 'skipped'.

I am greatly indebted to J. Strugnell, my colleague in the study of Cave IV fragments, who offered to translate my work. Beyond the normal responsibilities of a translator he discussed the revision sentence by sentence with me, and these discussions often led to more extensive changes in the book. To him, and to his wife who typed the whole and also drew up the concluding indexes, I would like to offer my best thanks. I also thank my colleague F. M. Cross Jr. who sent me the proofs of his work *The Ancient Library of Qumran* for use in my revision. The list of those who kindly put their photographs at my disposal is to be found in the index to the plates; my thanks are due to them all and in special degree to the Palestine Archaeological Museum and M. l'Abbé J. Starcky for the great help they gave me in making possible the photographic section of this book.

Discoveries in the Judaean Wilderness have not yet ceased. I write these lines in the camp of 'Ain Fešḫa where the latest campaign directed by R. P. R. de Vaux, O.P., and Dr A. Dajani is uncovering the remains of a considerable Essene agricultural settlement. Conclusions at this stage are still liable to modification, but I trust it will be of some use to have attempted a synthesis of all the evidence that has so far come to hand.

'Ain Fešḫa,
7 February 1958

J. T. MILIK

7

LIST OF ILLUSTRATIONS

MAPS

The Wilderness of Judaea (*facing title page*)
The Qumrân region (*facing page* 16)
Plan of the ruins of Ḥirbet Qumrân (*facing page* 48)

PLATES

We should like to express our thanks to the following for permission to reproduce the illustrations:

The Palestine Archaeological Museum: Plates 2, 3, 5–8, 10–13, 18–25.
M. l'Abbé J. Starcky: Plates 1, 4 and 14.
The Musad Bialik, Jerusalem: Plates 16 and 17.
The American Schools of Oriental Research: Plate 15.
The Biblical Archaeologist: Plate 9.

LIST OF ABBREVIATIONS

Ant.: Flavius Josephus, *Jewish Antiquities.*

BA: *Biblical Archaeologist.*

BASOR: *Bulletin of the American Schools of Oriental Research.*

CD: *Damascus Document* (Zadokite Fragments); MSS from the Cairo Geniza.

Discoveries . . . I: D. BARTHÉLEMY, O.P., and J. T. MILIK, *Qumran Cave I* (Discoveries in the Judaean Desert, I), Oxford 1955.

JBL: *Journal of Biblical Literature.*

JNES: *The Journal of Near Eastern Studies.*

Library: F. M. CROSS, *The Ancient Library of Qumran and Modern Biblical Studies,* New York, 1958.

LXX: Septuagint.

MT: Masoretic Text.

'Oṣar: E. L. SUKENIK and N. AVIGAD, *'Oṣar Hammegillot Haggenûzôt,* Jerusalem 1954.

PEQ: *Palestine Exploration Quarterly,* formerly the *Palestine Exploration Fund Quarterly Statement.*

RB: *Revue Biblique.*

TWNT: Kittel, *Theologisches Wörterbuch zum Neuen Testament,* Stuttgart, 1933 ff.

VT: *Vetus Testamentum.*

War: Flavius Josephus, *Jewish War.*

ZAW: *Zeitschrift für die Alttestamentliche Wissenschaft.*

Abbreviations used for the principal non-biblical manuscripts from Cave I:

1Q H: *Hôdayôt,* or *Hymns of Thanksgiving.*
1Q pHab: *Pešer,* or *Commentary on, Habakkuk.*
1Q M: *Serek hammilḥamah,* or *The Rule of the War.*
1Q S: *Serek hayyaḥad,* or *The Rule of the Community.*

I

THE STORY OF THE DISCOVERIES

A CLIFF 1,100 feet high towers above the north-western corner of the Dead Sea; its upper edge is level with the Mediterranean and marks off the eastern limit of the plateau called the Wilderness of Judaea. Its impressive reddish limestone face is honeycombed with countless natural caves, and, at its foot, a terrace of marl spreads out and falls away towards the Dead Sea, 1,292 feet below sea level. Long ages ago, the entire bed of the Jordan valley was covered with water, and the salt deposited at that time makes the soil barren even now.[1] In the spring, however, a little vegetation appears and then the semi-nomad Taʿâmireh tribe brings its sheep and goats down into the valley. They can water the flocks at ʿAin Fešḫa, a strongly flowing but brackish spring lying to the south of the area (cf. Frontispiece). Towards its centre, this area is divided by the course of a seasonal torrent, the Wadi Qumrân: a group of ruins on the terrace of marl to its left is called analogously Ḫirbet Qumrân (the word 'ḫirbeh' means 'ruin').[2]

THE FIRST MANUSCRIPT CAVE OF THE QUMRÂN AREA (1Q)

It was spring 1947. A shepherd, Moḥammad ed-Di'b (Mohammed the Wolf), was looking for a goat that had wandered off among the rocky slopes of the cliff, but, being rather weary, he sat down in the shade of a hollow in the rock. To amuse himself, he threw a stone into a hole in the cliff-face in front of him (Plate 1). A sound of something breaking came from inside and he took to his heels in fright. But curiosity was stronger than fear,

[1] Till the end of the Riss pluvial period, about 180,000 years ago, the level of water in the Jordan valley was about 600 ft above its present level.

[2] The writer had proposed a phonetic evolution from 'Kalamôn', the Byzantine name for the region (cf. also Papyrôn, Josephus, *Ant.* XIV.ii, 33; *War*. I.vi, 130), to Qumrân. However, on historical grounds he now considers improbable attempts to explain the name as deriving from Hebrew or Greek: we need not expect to find pre-Arabic origins for the name. In a region desolate from Byzantine times onward, it is unlikely that traditional place names would survive (cf. F.M. Cross, *Library*, ch. II, n. 3).

and the next day he returned to the spot with his cousin, Aḥmad Moḥammad. The two Bedouins wormed their way through the hole into the cave and found it to be a narrow cavern, its floor strewn with potsherds. At the back stood a row of eight unbroken jars with their lids still on. These were empty, however, all but one out of which they took three rolls, one large and two smaller ones. Somewhat disappointed with their discovery, they wondered what to do with them. Finally, after some weeks, their uncle brought all they had taken from the cave to a Bethlehem antiquities dealer, one Ḥalîl Iskandar Šahîn.

In Bethlehem, the writing on the rolls was thought to be Syriac, and so they were taken to the Monophysite Syrian Convent of St Mark, in the Old City of Jerusalem. Meanwhile clandestine excavations began in the cave, and other rolls, in more or less good condition, together with several handfuls of fragments, were recovered from the débris. In the autumn of that same year 1947, Bedouins and antique-dealers were going round Jerusalem's learned institutions, offering their manuscripts at very reasonable prices. In December, the Hebrew University acquired three of them. It was E. L. Sukenik, a professor of that university, who was the first to recognize the very great age of these rolls, and to suspect that they might be of Essene origin.

Mar Athanasius Yeshue Samuel, Syrian Metropolitan in residence at St Mark's convent, had also bought four manuscripts, and in February 1948 he showed them to J. C. Trever and W. H. Brownlee, who were then at the American School of Oriental Research in Jerusalem. They too realized the exceptional importance of the discovery, and secured the Archbishop's permission to photograph his rolls.

But the situation in Palestine was rapidly deteriorating, and towards the end of the British mandate (15 May 1948), Mar Athanasius left with his manuscripts and finally arrived with them in the United States. He did not, however, find selling them on the American market as easy as he had hoped, and it was not until 1955 that they were finally purchased by the State of Israel for the respectable price of $250,000. They are to be housed in 'The Shrine of the Book' which is now being built in Jerusalem.

In July 1948, a truce brought a lull in the war between the Jews and the Arabs. Archaeologists were able to go over the area of

Qumrân, which lay within the frontier of the new kingdom of Jordan, and to look for the hiding-place where the manuscripts had been found. The search was started at the suggestion of Captain Lippens, a Belgian U.N. observer. Some soldiers of the Arab Legion were sent to look for the cave and succeeded in finding it towards the end of January 1949. It was only later that it received its now common title, Qumrân Cave I (1Q). Between 15 February and 5 March, the Jordanian Department of Antiquities, the École Biblique et Archéologique Française de Jérusalem, and the Palestine Archaeological Museum carried out a systematic clearing of the cave. This team, occasionally assisted by the American School of Oriental Research in Jerusalem, was to collaborate in exploring and excavating this and associated sites to the present day. The overall supervision of the work has been in the hands of G. Lankester Harding, Director until autumn 1956 of the Jordanian Department of Antiquities, and Father Roland de Vaux, O.P., director of the École Biblique et Archéologique Française.

Father D. Barthélemy, O.P., and the author of this book were asked to study the hundreds of manuscript fragments that were recovered by this first excavation or bought on the antiquities market. They were published in 1955, together with the other objects found in the cave (pottery, cloth, etc.) in the first volume of a series called *Discoveries in the Judaean Desert* (Oxford University Press). As early as 1950–1, the American School had published three of the manuscripts that were at that time in the possession of Mar Athanasius Yeshue Samuel: the complete scroll of Isaiah (abbreviation: 1Q Is^a; Plate 9), the Habakkuk Commentary (abbreviation: 1Q pHab, *p* being the first letter of the Hebrew word *pešer*); the 'Rule of the Community' (abbreviation: 1 Q S, where *S* comes from the Hebrew title *Serek hayyaḥad*) entitled by its first editors 'The Manual of Discipline' (Plate 15). The first scrolls bought by the Israelis were partially published and discussed by E. L. Sukenik in two preliminary reports. His complete edition of the three manuscripts appeared posthumously at the end of 1954; it contained 'The Rule for the War' (*Serek hammilḥamah*, abbreviation 1Q M) called by Sukenik 'The War of the Children of Light against the Children of Darkness' (Plate 17); a collection of hymns (*Hodayot*, abbreviation

1Q H; Plate 16); and a fragmentary scroll of Isaiah (abbreviation 1Q Is*b*). The seventh and last scroll of Qumrân Cave I has recently been unrolled in the Hebrew University, Jerusalem. It is an Aramaic apocryphal work which gives an expanded version of the first fifteen chapters of Genesis. A preliminary publication of five of its columns appeared in 1956 with the not too appropriate title 'A Genesis Apocryphon'.[1,2]

DISCOVERIES AT MURABBA'ÂT. CAVES II AND III AT QUMRÂN

While the archaeologists were engaged, in December 1951, in the first season of excavation at Ḥirbet Qumrân, the Ta'âmireh brought to Jerusalem another group of manuscripts. This lot had been discovered towards the end of the preceding summer in caves in the Wadi Murabba'ât, about fifteen miles ESE of Jerusalem. It was later established that most of the documents found there dated from the Second Jewish Revolt (A.D. 132–5).

Between 21 January and 3 March of the following year, the institutions that we have mentioned above excavated these caves and recovered further documents as well as other objects which enabled them to establish that there had been four phases of

[1]B. Mazar *ap.* D. Flusser (*Kirjath Sepher* XXXII, p. 579, n. 3) has more plausibly proposed to call it *Sefer 'abôt*, 'The Book of the Patriarchs'. An Aramaic title, *Ketâb 'abāhān*, would be more appropriate.

[2]The first news of the discoveries of 1947 reached Europe at the beginning of 1948, and were received by scholars with a certain scepticism. This was soon dispelled after the excavation of Cave I and the discoveries that followed thereupon. The intransigent position of a scholar like S. Zeitlin, editor of the *Jewish Quarterly Review*, no longer deserves serious consideration. Despite occasionally violent discussions, agreement was soon reached on several disputed questions. For instance, scholars are now agreed in dating the manuscripts roughly between the second century B.C. and the first century A.D., although originally authorities like P. Kahle and G. R. Driver had proposed far later dates. Again, the hypothesis that the scrolls had been stored away in the caves and that Ḥirbet Qumrân had been destroyed during the course of the First Jewish Revolt (A.D. 66–70) were soon accepted by the scholarly world, even though at the beginning theories had fluctuated between the Hellenistic period and the Middle Ages. Likewise there is general agreement in identifying, broadly speaking, the inhabitants of Qumrân with the Essenes, and such hypotheses as that they were Pharisees, Sadducees, disciples of St John the Baptist, Qaraites, etc. are being set aside. Discussion now centres especially on the following points: narrowing the chronological limits in which the origins of the sect are to be put; delimiting the external (Greek and Persian) influences on Essene doctrine and practice; and circumscribing the Essene influences on the doctrines, institutions and literary form of the New Testament.

occupation: Chalcolithic (4000–3000 B.C.), Middle Bronze (2000–1600 B.C.), Iron II (eighth and seventh centuries B.C.), and Greco-Roman. It is noteworthy that this was the first time that ancient objects in perishable materials, such as wooden vessels or the remains of rush mats, had been found in Palestine.

About the same time, February 1952, the indefatigable Ta-'âmireh came back to the Qumrân area, and found there a second cave containing manuscripts (2Q) a little to the south of the first one; however, there were only a few handfuls of fragments to be recovered from it and their content was of the same type as that of the Cave I manuscripts. The reaction of the archaeologists was not long in coming; between 10 and 22 March, the École Biblique, the American School and the Palestine Museum investigated every cave and hollow that they could find in the cliffs for five miles around Qumrân (see the line of crosses between Ḥajar Eṣba' and Ras Fešḫa, on Map 1; Map 2 shows the site of each cave). Over a score of caves were found to contain fragments of pottery like that from Cave I and the Ḥirbeh.[1] Further, the archaeologists unexpectedly discovered a third cave containing manuscripts, two of which were rolls of copper. The text was engraved on them in Hebrew square letters, a few of which could be read in relief on the back of the rolled strips of metal.

ḤIRBET MIRD AND A CACHE FROM THE SECOND REVOLT

The discovery of Cave III was not to be the last of the year 1952. Towards the middle of July, the Bedouins made a new find at Ḥirbet Mird, nine miles south-east of Jerusalem. This time the manuscripts came from an old monastery called, in Byzantine writings, *Castellion* or *Marda*. This latter name is Aramaic and means the same as the first, 'fortress': the monastery was built on the site of the Hasmonean fortress Hyrcanion. The remains of its library were recovered from an underground chamber, and consisted of manuscripts in three languages: Arabic, Greek and Christian Palestinian Aramaic (i.e. the dialect used by the Christians of Palestine in the Byzantine period and during the first centuries of Arab domination). Palaeographical criteria lead one to date all these texts towards the end of the Byzantine and the

[1] See Additional Note 1.

beginning of the Arab periods. An Arabic contract contains a date in the second century of the Hegira (eighth century A.D.). On 2 August, the first of these documents was purchased and the University of Louvain charged Professor de Langhe and Captain Lippens with the direction of a 'Mission Archéologique Belge' to work at the site between February and April 1953. Excavation of the underground chamber brought to light further fragments of the same type.

It was in July 1952 that the Ta'âmireh offered for sale in Jerusalem documents coming from caves which it is hard to pinpoint geographically. On 5 August, a first lot was bought containing, among other things, Nabatean papyri (Plate 24); on 22 and 23 August further groups were acquired, including fragments of a Greek translation of the Hebrew text of the Twelve Minor Prophets. Also found were fragments of the Hebrew Bible and some Greek and Aramaic (Plate 25) documents. The group is to be dated towards the end of the first and the beginning of the second century A.D.: the *terminus ad quem* is the Second Jewish Revolt, for it was then that these documents were hidden in their caves.

QUMRÂN CAVES IV, V AND VI

The most sensational discovery, after that of Cave I, took place at the beginning of September 1952, and its story may seem even more extraordinary. One evening in one of their tents, a group of Ta'âmireh were discussing the recent finds which were winning them world-wide fame . . . and a substantial income. A remark roused a venerable grey-beard from his somnolence, calling his mind back to something which might be of interest to keen cave-hunters. It happened long ago, during his youth, he explained, when he was hunting in the region of Qumrân. He was following a wounded partridge when, suddenly, it disappeared into a hole not far from the ruins. With great difficulty, he reached his prey which had fallen into a cave, and there he collected also an old terra-cotta lamp and a few potsherds. The younger tribesmen noted carefully the topographical details that the old man gave, equipped themselves with a bag of flour, ropes and primitive lamps, and went down to Qumrân. Using their ropes, they finally climbed into the right cave (Plate 3) and set to sifting its earth. They had already turned over several cubic metres of earth when, suddenly, their hands came upon a compact layer of thousands of manuscript fragments. Their courage and perseverance had its reward.

Some weeks later, the Bedouins began the round of visits to the various archaeological institutes of Jerusalem. Naturally they gave false clues, for they hoped to be able to continue their fruitful excavation in peace. But other tribesmen were jealous of the lucky finders and soon the exact whereabouts of the cave was known. Mounted police from Jericho set out for the site, and their appearance caused the unauthorized excavators to flee. On 22 September, Father de Vaux and the author, who had already taken part in the cave survey during March, took over from the Bedouins, and, for a week, with the help of the Department of Antiquities and the Museum, uncovered several hundred more manuscript fragments. Looking into some near-by cracks in the rocks, they increased their booty with the remains of a dozen manuscripts from another cave, although these were unfortunately half decayed by dampness. This cave received the number five, while the 'partridge' cave was numbered IV. Both of them had been artificially hollowed out of the terrace of marl, while the earlier caves, which were further removed from the ruin, lay in the limestone cliff itself.

At the foot of the cliff, a further hole was identified at this time, Cave VI, from which a small wad of fragments had come that had already been bought by the Palestine Museum on 13 September.

As for the manuscript fragments that the Bedouins had unearthed in Cave IV, they could only be bought lot by lot, and negotiations for the purchase of the last of them still have to be concluded. Considerable sums of money were called for, and an appeal was made to the learned institutions of the whole world. In addition to the Jordanian Government which contributed £15,000, McGill University in Montreal, the Universities of Manchester and Heidelberg, McCormick Theological Seminary in Chicago, and the Vatican Library offered financial help in acquiring these fragments. All this material, apart from a few fragments in the hands of private persons, is, at the moment, kept together in the Palestine Archaeological Museum in Jerusalem (Jordan).

The amount of material discovered in Cave IV called for the work of a team of scholars to prepare it for publication, and it was decided that this team should be international and interconfessional. Here are the names of its members: Mgr P. W. Skehan, Professor at the Catholic University of America, Washington; F. M. Cross, Jr., now Professor at the Harvard Divinity School; J. M. Allegro, Lecturer at the University of Manchester; the Abbé J. Starcky, of the Centre National de la Recherche Scientifique, Paris; J. Strugnell, of Jesus College, Oxford; C. H. Hunzinger, Dozent at the University of Göttingen, and the present writer, who is also associated with the Centre National de la Recherche Scientifique.

The fragments of Caves II, III, VI and VII–X (cf. *infra*) will be published by the Abbé M. Baillet, Professor at the Institut Catholique in Toulouse, and the writer has further been made responsible for the publication of the fragments of Cave V, together with the copper rolls from Cave III. The latter were opened by Professor H. Wright Baker of the Manchester Technological Institute in the beginning of 1956. All the manuscripts will be published in the series *Discoveries in the Judaean Desert*, which has already been mentioned, and which will contain at least ten volumes. The one devoted to the discoveries in the Wadi Murabba'ât will be the second in the series, and should be published before long.

QUMRÂN CAVES VII–XI AND A NEW CAVE AT MURABBA'ÂT

The year 1952 thus proved to be exceptionally fruitful, but it did not mark the end of the discoveries. We have alluded to the seasons of excavation at Ḥirbet Qumrân: during the fourth of these, in the spring of 1955, four new caves (VII–X) were discovered in the side of the marl terrace on which the ruins stand. These caves, however, were almost completely destroyed by erosion and produced unfortunately only a few fragments of manuscripts and one ostracon (inscribed potsherd).

About the same time, a Ta'âmireh shepherd found in a small cave in the Wadi Murabba'ât, a much damaged scroll. Nevertheless, it contained a substantial part of the biblical text of the Twelve Minor Prophets, between the end of Joel and the beginning of Zechariah. It dates from the beginning of the second century A.D.

Lastly, at the start of 1956, the Bedouins, who were carrying on their own survey of every smallest crack in the vast cliff, found an eleventh cave with manuscripts (Plate 4), comparable in importance to Caves I and IV. This discovery strengthens some scholars in their opinion that the dry Judaean Desert promises still more treasures with which to cool their thirst for discovery.[1]

To sum up, the discoveries of manuscripts in the Judaean Desert can be divided into three groups on the basis both of their date and their provenance: (1) Manuscripts coming from the caves in the Qumrân area, in the vicinity of the community settlement at Ḥirbet Qumrân, dating, broadly speaking, from the second century B.C. to the first century A.D. (2) Documents from Murabbaʿât and another unidentified site, found in caves in wadis that are hard of access and remote from all centres of habitation, in the southern part of the Judaean Desert. These caves served as refuges in all periods, but were especially so used during the Second Jewish Revolt. (3) Manuscripts found in the ruins of a Byzantine monastery, Ḥirbet Mird. This lay not far from Jerusalem, in the middle of the 'monks' desert', which knew its greatest days in the fifth and sixth centuries of our era.[2]

[1] For accounts of the discovery of Cave I by those chiefly involved, see J. C. Trever, *BA* XI, 1948, pp. 46–57; Mar Athanasius, *BA* XII, 1949, pp. 26–31; E. L. Sukenik, *'Oṣar*, pp. 13–17; Y. Yadin, *The Message of the Scrolls*, pp. 15–30; Mohammed Eddi'b, in *JNES* XVI, pp. 236–7. G. L. Harding, in *Discoveries . . .*, I, pp. 3–7, gives a summary based on intensive cross-examinations of the Arab principals; F. M. Cross, *Library*, ch. I, discusses the various accounts critically. For other discoveries in the Judaean Desert and the work of publication, see *RB* LX, 1953, pp. 19 ff.; 83–88; 245–8; 540–61; LXI, 1954, p. 161, and especially *RB* LXIII, 1956, pp. 49–67 (in English, *BA* XIX, 1956, pp. 75–96) and *VT* Suppl. IV, 1957, pp. 17 ff. On the excavations at Murabbaʿât, see R. de Vaux, *RB* LX, 1953, pp. 245–75.

[2] Some earlier discoveries of manuscripts in the region of Jericho should be mentioned. According to a colophon in Origen's Hexapla, a Greek version of the Psalms together with other Greek and Hebrew manuscripts were found in a jar near Jericho, during the reign of Caracalla (Mercati, *Studi e Testi* 5, Rome 1901, pp. 28 ff.). The finding of 'books of the Old Testament and other books in Hebrew writing' in a cave in the region of Jericho, about the year 785, is recorded in a letter from the Nestorian Patriarch Timotheus I (*ob.* 823) to Sergius the Metropolitan of Elam (cf. *Discoveries . . .* p. 88, n. 4; and for the date, R.S. Bidawid, *Les Lettres du Patriarche Nestorien, Timothée I, Studi e Testi* 187, 1956, p. 71). It is possible that a manuscript of the Pentateuch, often cited by the Massoretes and called the 'Jericho Pentateuch', came from a similar discovery.

II

THE QUMRÂN LIBRARY

So far, the caves of Qumrân have produced parts of almost 600 manuscripts, but only ten or so rolls have been preserved complete, and some texts are only represented by one fragment. When we look for a reason for these deposits, it seems most plausible to connect the storing of the manuscripts in caves with the clearly attested Roman destruction of the settlement, and we may consequently neglect the view that we are dealing here with a Geniza[1] or storing place for worn-out manuscripts. Little attention, however, has so far been paid to the various types of deposit; taking the material evidence in conjunction with the manuscripts themselves, we may suggest a provisional classification into three categories:

(1) Cave IV seems to contain the main library of the convent. The cave itself is artificial, and the character of the pottery found there shows that it had once served as a cell for a hermit. The scrolls had been piled up in it so densely as practically to fill one of its two chambers. The lack of jars or of other arrangements for storing so many manuscripts suggests that they had been left there in a hurry. It probably was chosen as a hiding place because of its proximity to the settlement; and the occasion on which it was filled, to judge from the palaeographical date of the latest manuscript found there, is most probably the threatened Roman attack. The extremely fragmentary state of the manuscripts, the fact that some of the tears in the manuscripts are indubitably old, and the survival of long strips that seem to have been torn off the rolls, all seem to indicate a violation of the cave in antiquity. We may place this fairly near in time to the date of deposit of the manuscripts, as a thick layer of dust forms rapidly in the cave and would soon have hidden the scrolls from damage by man or beast.

[1] On Genizas, cf. *The Jewish Encyclopedia*, V, 1903, p. 612; P. E. Kahle, *The Cairo Geniza*, London 1947, p. 2.

Two other types of caves containing numerically less important groups of manuscripts are to be distinguished:

(2) Cave I is a good example of one type. Its narrow interior, and the difficulty of access, exclude the possibility that it was a hermit's cell; it could serve only as a hiding place. But the fact that the remains of nearly eighty manuscripts and about fifty jars were found in it shows that it served as hiding place or storage cave for several hermitages; close by it, to the south, there is a cluster of caves which show traces of occupation during the Roman period (see Map 2). In the same category, we should probably put Cave III; fragments of several dozen jars were found there, although the cave had collapsed, and time has dealt hardly with the several dozen manuscripts that come from it.

(3) All other caves in which manuscripts were found belong to the third type of cave. These were inhabited by individual hermits: the manuscripts and domestic utensils in the keeping of each hermit were found as he left them when he abandoned his cave. Typical cases are Caves V and XI. Cave V is artificially hollowed out of the marl terrace, with a well-formed entrance and smooth floor. In it, fragments of manuscripts were found neatly piled in a corner. Cave XI, easy of access, opens on to a small terrace facing the Dead Sea. It has a small antechamber which could easily serve for living quarters—the archaeological data confirm this—and in a chamber behind this, manuscripts and other objects were stored.

HOW THE SCROLLS WERE WRITTEN

In the writing of scrolls, two materials were used. The less extensively preserved is papyrus. Locally grown reeds from Lake Huleh in Galilee or near-by Kalamôn may have been used, although perhaps better quality papyrus was imported from Egypt. A microscopic analysis may enable one to decide which sort was used. But more often leather scrolls or fragments have been found. Analysis reveals that 'sheep-like' and 'goat-like' skins were used, which may have been tanned at Qumrân (although a tannery has not yet been identified with any plausibility;[1] the functions of many of the industrial installations are still obscure) or brought already prepared from Jerusalem or Jericho (although

[1]See Additional Note 2.

on grounds of ritual purity this is less probable). In quality, the skins vary from a fine, thin leather, smoothed on both sides and very light in colour, to a dark, crudely prepared stuff.

The leather was usually inscribed on the hair-side, but sometimes the less worn parts of damaged scrolls were turned upside down and re-used. The scribe will have considered the length and character of his text, calculated the length and height of scroll that he would need, and then chosen skins of an appropriate size and quality. The main work of copying was done in the monastery at Qumrân in a spacious room, the scriptorium (cf. p. 48), found above the ground floor and probably open to one side. The scribes sat in it, squatting before long narrow tables (Plate 11). In addition to his sheet of papyrus or leather, each scribe shared with his neighbour a small table on which was kept a big supply of reed pens (probably cut from the near-by marshes), and cylindrical inkstands. The ink used was (with some possible exceptions) of a purely vegetable composition, of a consistency approximating to that of modern India ink. Before writing on a skin, the scribe traced column margins and lines with a stylus. Each skin usually contained three or four columns. When writing the text, he suspended each letter from the lines traced. In the later period of scribal activity represented at Qumrân, the letters are written at a certain distance below the line; by the time of the second Jewish Revolt, they have dropped to half-way between the two lines. A book can be copied in two possible ways, from dictation or from a written examplar before the scribe's eyes. Probably both methods were used at Qumrân, as certain modes of spelling are more easily explained as errors of hearing or of pronunciation, others as slips of the eye. Perhaps, as was normal in Greek copying houses, several scribes were engaged in making copies, while one man read a scroll.

Either by degrees, or more probably after completing the work, the scribe himself, or sometimes a corrector, checked the copy against its archetype. Additions or erroneous spellings were rarely erased; normally, dots were put above and below the wrong letters, and the corrections or additions were inserted above the line. In the case of a long addition, it overflows the line and runs vertically down the margin.

The final phase was the gluing together of the papyrus sheets, or the sewing together of the skins of leather, to make the complete scroll. Each roll was then rolled round a stick of wood, and the title either inscribed on the back of the outer sheet or written on a special label sewn on to one end of the scroll. The outer edge of the scroll was most liable to damage from use, and to this is due the loss of almost all the original titles of works from Qumrân. Finally, the roll was wrapped in linen cloth, and either piled up or put in a clay receptacle.

The size of the scrolls varied greatly. The extremes ranged from 8 metres by 60 centimetres (1Q Is*a*) to tiny scrolls not higher than 8 centimetres (several examples of the latter come from Cave IV, but their fragmentary state rarely permits us to know their length).

There is some evidence that scribes were trained within the community. An ostracon was found inscribed with an alphabet in a clumsy attempt to write in the Qumrân book-hand. This may be interpreted as a learner's exercise, and would agree with the economic independence of the Essene community and its education of youths reported by classical writers.

BIBLICAL MANUSCRIPTS: THE TORAH

A quarter of the manuscripts consists of copies of books of the Bible or, to be more precise, of books which after the end of the first century A.D. were considered canonical by the Jews of Palestine. Only the Book of Esther fails to appear, while works like Deuteronomy, Isaiah, the Minor Prophets and the Psalms are represented by more than ten copies. It is noteworthy that some of the copies of biblical books found at Qumrân are relatively close in date to the original autographs. For instance, a manuscript of Daniel from the fourth cave is only half a century removed from the date of composition of the original (*circa* 164 B.C.). Only a century separates the manuscript of Ecclesiastes which is shown in Plate 7 from the author's copy. Occurrences of this kind are rare, even with Egyptian papyri containing the texts of classical writers.

Specialists in the textual criticism of the Old Testament naturally expect much from these new manuscripts. If the biblical scrolls from Cave I failed to overturn the results of earlier scholarly investigation, texts from Cave IV will at least put some of them in question. Let us take a few examples.

As for the Pentateuch, the Masoretic text is found in most of the new fragments. Among the exceptions, however, we should note a copy of Exodus (4Q Ex*ᵃ*) which is related to the Hebrew text underlying the Septuagint. F. M. Cross has reconstructed the first six verses of Exodus according to this manuscript as follows: '[These are the names of the children of Israel who came to Egypt] with Jacob *their father*, each with his household. [There came Reuben, Simeon, Levi and Judah,] Issachar, Zebulun, *Joseph* and Benjamin; Dan [and Naphtali, Gad and Asher; all the *offspring of Jacob* (?) were] seventy-*five persons*. (. . .) Then Joseph died . . .' In these verses, as Cross observes, 'no fewer than six certain variants are to be found. . . . Four readings are in agreement with the LXX; one is unique . . .; and one probably agrees with the MT against LXX.'[1] The variant number given for Joseph's family is familiar to readers of the New Testament, where it is found in St Stephen's speech (Acts 7.14).

Other manuscripts which have been proved to be very close to the LXX are a copy of Numbers (4Q Num*ᵇ*) and a small roll which contains only the Song of Moses (Deut. 32) (Plate 6). As an example we cite a verse from the Song of Moses giving its forms according to the LXX, 4Q, and the Masoretic Text.[2]

Deut. 32.43:

LXX	4 Qumrân	MT
Exult, *O heavens*, with him	Exult, *O heavens*, with him	Exult, *O peoples*, with him
Adore him, all ye *sons of God*	Adore him, all ye *Gods*	[*vocalization corrected*]
Exult, O peoples, with his people		
Magnify him, all ye angels of God		
For the blood of his *children*, he will avenge (it)	For the blood of his *children*, he will avenge (it)	For the blood of his *servants*, he will avenge (it)
he will avenge it and be revenged of his enemies	*And he will be revenged of* his enemies	*And he will be revenged of* his enemies
Those who hate him, he will repay them	Those who hate him, he will repay them	
And *the Lord* will purify *the land of his people*	And *he* will purify *the land of his people*	And *he* will purify *his land (and) his people*

[1] F. M. Cross, *Library*, pp. 137 f.
[2] P. W. Skehan, *BASOR* 136, Dec. 1954, pp. 12 ff.; Cross, *op cit.*, pp. 135–7.

In another manuscript of Exodus we come into contact with the recension found in the Samaritan Pentateuch. It is written in palaeo-Hebrew characters (Plate 5) which are the continuation of the old Phoenician alphabet and the source of the Samaritan script. Samaritan-type readings are also found in the manuscript of Numbers (4Q Num*b*), mentioned above.

THE FORMER PROPHETS

Of this group, which comprises the books of Joshua, Judges, Samuel and Kings, examples have been found in four of the caves at Qumrân. They seem to be derived from the same Hebrew tradition as is represented in the LXX. This is especially clear in the case of a manuscript of Samuel (4Q Sam*a*), whose fragments give us samples from every chapter of the work. A strip of papyrus was applied to the back of the scroll in antiquity to strengthen the leather and this helped to preserve it. The scroll originally contained 57 columns (33 for I Sam., 24 for II Sam.) and the type of text copied, as well as the way in which it was arranged in the various columns, can be restored for the greater part of the book. Cross has suggested that the author of Chronicles used a text of Samuel closer to that of 4Q Sam*a* than to that of the Masoretic text.

Another Samuel manuscript deserves mention here (4Q Sam*b*). According to Cross, who has published a detailed palaeographic study of it, its script would date it towards the end of the third century B.C.; it and 4Q Ex*f* are rivals for the title of the oldest of all known biblical manuscripts. Although the extremely fragmentary state of the MS scarcely permits us to be certain, the text represented seems to be superior, in places, to both LXX and MT. I Sam. 23.10–13 may be cited as an example (Plate 19).[1]

4Q	LXX	MT
[And David said: 'O Yahweh God of Israel,] thy servant has heard definitely that Saul seeks [to come to Keilah, to wreck the city on my	And David said: 'O Yahweh God of Israel, thy servant has heard definitely that Saul seeks to come to Keilah to wreck the city on	And David said: 'O Yahweh God of Israel, thy servant has heard definitely that Saul seeks to come to Keilah to wreck the city on my account.

[1]F. M. Cross *JBL* LXXIV, 1955, pp. 169 ff.

account. (- - -)

And now will Saul
come down as thy
servant has
heard? O Yahweh,]
God of Israel, *tell*
thy servant'. [*And
Yahweh said: 'He will
come down.' Then
David said. 'Will the
citizens of Keilah de-
liver me and my men
into the land of Sa]ul'?
And Yahweh said:
'They will del[iver.'*

So arose David and *his*
men,
about 400 men, and
they departed from
Keilah, and they
went about where-
ever they could.

Then it was told to Sau]l
that David had es-
caped from Keilah,
[so he gave up his
raid.]

my account.

And now will Saul
come down as thy
servant has
heard? O Yahweh,
God of Israel, *tell*
thy servant.'

*And Yahweh said: 'It
will be shut up.'*

So arose David and *the
men who were with him,*
about 400 men, and
they departed from
Keilah, and they
went about wherever
they could.

Then it was told to Saul
that David had es-
caped from Keilah,
so he gave up his
raid.

*Will the citizens of
Keilah deliver me into
his hand?* Will Saul
come down as
thy servant hath
heard? O Yahweh,
God of Israel, *pray
tell* thy servant.' *And
Yahweh said: 'He will
come down.' Then
David said: 'Will the
citizens of Keilah de-
liver me and my men
into the hand of Saul?'
And Yahweh said:
'They will deliver.'*

So arose David and *his*
men,
about 600 men, and
they departed from
Keilah, and they
went about wherever
they could.

And to Saul it was told
that David had es-
caped from Keilah,
so he gave up his
raid.

THE LATTER PROPHETS

The Three Major Prophets (Isaiah, Jeremiah and Ezekiel) and
the Twelve Minor Prophets are well represented among the
manuscripts from Qumrân. Isaiah is easily the most frequently
found. Two almost complete rolls were discovered in the first
cave, the second of which (1Q Is*b*) reflects faithfully the tradition
that the Masoretes preserved; and the same could be said of a
dozen fragmentary manuscripts of the same prophet which were
found in Cave IV (Plate 20). On the other hand, the other Isaiah
scroll from Cave I (1Q Is*a*) shows the characteristics of a more
popular edition (Plate 9): its spelling is fuller, so that it becomes
easier to read, and certain changes in the text seem to have been
introduced under the influences of developing Messianic doctrines. One detail is of some significance: chapter 33 finishes

towards the foot of column XXVII, and the three ruled lines which follow are left blank. Furthermore, the sheet on which it is written has only two columns instead of the four that are usual in this roll. Chapter 34 begins on a new sheet of leather, and the text thereafter continues without further interruption until the end of the book. This oddity may well indicate that there persisted a memory of two different collections of prophecies (corresponding roughly to the modern distinction between Proto- and Deutero-Isaiah), although the two collections had already been combined into one book by the time of the copyist.[1]

Here too, the LXX type of text is found in one case: in Jeremiah, this text is one eighth shorter than the Masoretic text, and all the fragments of 4Q Jer*b* follow the shorter form. For instance, in chapter 10, the LXX omits four verses and places a fifth in a different order; the Qumrân manuscript follows it in all these particulars. For Ezekiel and the Twelve Minor Prophets, the textual variants are no less interesting, but, on the whole, these manuscripts all belong to the Masoretic tradition.

THE WRITINGS

The Qumrân manuscripts of the *Kethûbîm* or Writings also cast new light on certain problems of textual criticism. The Book of Job has been identified in two fragmentary manuscripts, one of them in the normal square characters and the other in the palaeo-Hebrew script. This gives support to a suggestion once made by F. Delitzsch, that if its archetype had been written in the palaeo-Hebrew script, many difficulties and corruptions in the Masoretic text could be explained. To these witnesses we can now add extensive fragments of an Aramaic translation of Job found in Cave XI. At least these will show us how this difficult text was understood at a very early period in its history.

There are a dozen fragmentary scrolls of the Psalms, some of which, however, never contained more than Ps. 119, written out stichometrically and alphabetically. Apart from copies of this psalm, a stichometric arrangement is found in only one other manuscript from Cave IV. At least two scrolls from Cave IV and

---

[1] There are, furthermore, differences in grammar and orthography between the two parts, and the material disposition of the text in the roll is not the same.

one from Cave XI give the Psalms in an order different from that of the Masoretes.[1]

The Book of Daniel was much read. Two manuscripts of it were found in Cave I, four in Cave IV, and one in Cave VI. They follow the Masoretic text, apart from a few variants related to the Hebrew archetype of the LXX. Fragments from Caves I and IV give us the verses where the language changes from Hebrew to Aramaic (2.4) and from Aramaic back to Hebrew (8.1) just as in the Masoretic text; so there is nothing new that can be added on that irritating problem.[2]

THE HEBREW OF THE BIBLICAL TEXT: NEW DATA

The *Mishnah* informs us that the Rabbis, who after the destruction of Jerusalem founded a type of academy in Jamnia, fixed in about A.D. 100 the text of the Torah with the help of three manuscripts which had been saved from the Temple. This was done in a somewhat mechanical way; the reading attested by two manuscripts was systematically preferred to that preserved by only one.[3] The same method was probably used also for the other books of the Palestinian Canon. The Rabbis certainly had very old manuscripts available to them, since manuscripts at that time were carefully copied and preserved, especially in 'academic' circles; a few copies in the Qumrân library date back even to the third century B.C. For the text of the Former Prophets, they used less carefully written texts than those of the Hebrew archetypes of the LXX. At Qumrân the Writings are copied with more freedom than is found in the other sections of the Bible, a situation to be explained by the later date at which some of them were composed and by the fact that they did not have a long history of transmission such as would lead to the establishment of clearly defined text-types. Having established the text of the Holy Books, the Jews of Palestine seem to have set about eliminating all diverging recensions.

[1]Cf. J. T. Milik, *Biblica* XXXVIII, 1957, pp. 245 ff.

[2]On the biblical texts of Cave IV, see the preliminary report of F. M. Cross and P. W. Skehan in *RB* LXIII, 1956, pp. 56–60, and for further detail, P. W. Skehan, *VT* Suppl. IV, 1957, pp. 148 ff., and F. M. Cross, *Library*, ch. IV.

[3]*Ta'anit* IV, 2; *Sopherim* VI, 4; cf. A. Geiger, *Urschrift und Uebersetzungen der Bibel*², Frankfurt 1928, pp. 232–51.

The Hebrew manuscripts from Qumrân are thus unique, not only in their age, but also in their text. Through them we have direct information about a period that is of capital importance for the history of the Bible, the period immediately preceding the establishment of the consonantal text. Fragments from the Murabba'ât caves and from an unidentified site (dating from the Second Jewish Revolt) provide a marked contrast. In these manuscripts we find a text *identical* with that of the Masoretes, at least as far as our evidence goes (Pentateuch (Plate 18), Isaiah, Minor Prophets, and Psalms).

Contemporaneous with this process of canonization of books and texts, there was a 'canonization' of the script proper for biblical scrolls. At Qumrân, the Hebrew book-hand gives evidence of a rapid evolution, but the 'Masoretic' manuscripts of Murabba'ât show scarcely any development beyond the latest stage reached at Qumrân. Between this Murabba'ât script and that of medieval manuscripts, little change takes place. In contrast with the swift evolution of the script in the preceding three centuries, the normalized script henceforth develops at the slow pace proper to things ecclesiastical.

While the Rabbis at Jamnia thus checked further degeneration in the consonantal text of the Bible, the Samaritans of Shechem, where the modern village of Balata stands, near Nablus, confined their own Canon to the first five books. Their text of the Torah was based on some old manuscript containing a recension later than that followed by the Synod of Jamnia. The Samaritan schism, which cast its roots back into the Persian period, owes its origin to political rather than religious divergences. The struggle became particularly bitter towards the end of the second century B.C., with the military conquest of Shechem and the destruction of the temple on Mount Gerizim by John Hyrcanus. The Samaritans' limiting of the boundaries of the Canon to the books of the Pentateuch, and the copying of them in the palaeo-Hebrew script, were two of the many traits that made reconciliation with Rabbinic Judaism impossible. From the form of script used by the Samaritans for their Scriptures, we may conjecture that the final establishment of the material form of their text took place roughly contemporaneously with the recensional work of the Rabbis of Jamnia: the script now used by them is a stereotyped descendant from the form into which the palaeo-Hebrew script had evolved by about A.D. 100. It is plausible to suggest that, as in the case of the orthodox Canon, the establishment of the Samaritan Canon entailed also the 'canonization' of the form of script in which it was to be copied, so that palaeographic evolution became much slower. We may perhaps see in the choice of a script not easily read at that time an indication of the sacerdotal and closed nature of Samaritanism. In contrast to them, the Rabbis at Jamnia stipulated that for the writing of biblical scrolls the then current and easily readable 'square' script should be used. This indicates the more lay and democratic character of their movement.

We said that the Rabbis of about A.D. 100 suppressed the variety of recensions of biblical books that are attested in the Qumrân libraries. At this time, then, the text-forms that the LXX had followed disappeared. This measure separated Judaism still further from the Alexandrian Christians, and from the early Church in general, which had adopted as its own Bible the text of the LXX. It should be made clear that the Greek LXX was little used at Qumrân. In Cave IV only a few fragments of it were found, belonging to two manuscripts of Leviticus and to one of Numbers. Their script is of a type current in the first century B.C., but it could have continued in use in Palestine into the next century. The text in them is essentially the same as that found in other witnesses to the LXX, although, strikingly enough, in one of them the Tetragram is transliterated as IAÔ instead of being translated by *Kyrios*.[1] A manuscript found in the unidentified site in association with documents from the Second Revolt also comes from this period (late first century B.C.–early first century A.D.). It contains extensive sections of the Greek text of the Minor Prophets, apparently a revision of the LXX translation according to a Hebrew text closer to what was to become the standard Masoretic text. It seems that this version continued in circulation in the second century when Justin Martyr apparently quotes from it; indeed the Quinta of Origen's Hexapla is closely related to it.[2] These fragments from the Judaean Wilderness can

[1] P. Skehan, *VT* Suppl. IV, 1957, pp. 14 ff. Furthermore, some fragments of Exodus were found in Cave VII: *RB* LXIII, 1956, p. 572.

[2] Cf. D. Barthélemy, *RB* LX, 1953, pp. 18–29, and P. Kahle, *Theologische Literaturzeitung* 82, 1957, p. 648.

now be added to the occasional scraps of papyrus of the same date found in Egypt, to improve our knowledge of the earliest history of the LXX text.

There is little evidence from Qumrân for the existence of written Aramaic translations of the Bible (Targumim). This may be due to the fact that such translations were little needed in the highly educated milieu of the Essene community. The *Genesis Apocryphon* (cf. pp. 35 f.), even if it contains sections translated verbatim from the Hebrew of Genesis, is no true Targum nor Midrash. Rather it is an ambitious compilation of traditional lore concerning the Patriarchs, preserving the popular literary form of the pseudepigraph (the Patriarchs themselves being the narrators). Mention has been made of a Targum of Job found in Cave XI; nothing can yet be said of its technique of translation. But Job was already known to be peculiar in that both the LXX and rabbinical sources attest the existence of a written Targum of the book at a very early period.[1] Recently a few scraps of a verbatim Aramaic translation of Leviticus (16.12–15, 18–21) from Cave IV have been identified. The scroll, if complete, would have been of great importance for the lexical study of priestly terminology. For instance, it alone translates *kapporet* by *ksy'* (covering).

THE DEUTERO-CANONICAL BOOKS OR APOCRYPHA

It is well known that the canon of the Alexandrian Jews included certain additional books, which are also found in the liturgy and Bibles of the early Church. At Qumrân, examples of three of these books have been found: Tobit, Ecclesiasticus (or Ben Sira) and the Epistle of Jeremy. Three of the manuscripts of Tobit are in Aramaic and one in Hebrew. The author has been allotted these for study and a preliminary investigation suggests that Aramaic was the original language of the book. Both the Hebrew and Aramaic texts follow the longer recension, which is that attested by the Codex Sinaiticus and by the Vetus Latina. Sinaiticus is, however, corrupt, especially where *homoeoteleuton* causes two long omissions, and comparison with the Qumrân texts here supports the recension of the Vetus Latina; both are

---

[1] Cf. Job 42.17*b* (LXX), *T. b. Šab.* 115*a*, j. *Šab.* XVI, 1 and P. Kahle, *The Cairo Geniza*, pp. 123 ff.

often the only witnesses to certain readings, as, e.g. the *seven* sons of the young Tobiah (Tob. 14.3).

Among the fragments of Cave II, Abbé M. Baillet has identified a few scraps of the Hebrew original of Ecclesiasticus (6.20–31) which show a textual form practically identical with that of the manuscripts from the Cairo Geniza. Moreover, some small fragments of papyrus found in Cave VII seem to give part of the Epistle of Jeremy in Greek.[1]

OLD TESTAMENT PSEUDEPIGRAPHA: JUBILEES

A sizable section of the Qumrân manuscripts represent Pseudepigrapha of the Old Testament. Scholars had ascribed many of these works to the pre-Christian period, although they sometimes had to allow for the presence of Christian interpolations. This view is hard to defend in the light of the Qumrân data, where only one of the major Pseudepigrapha is found in the same textual form as underlies the early translations which were, until recently, our only witnesses to these works. This is the Book of Jubilees, which tells again the story of salvation from the Creation until the theophany of Mount Sinai.

The account of the origins of the chosen people is arranged in periods each forty-nine years long, and the number of periods itself is forty-nine, so that the whole forms a Jubilee of Jubilees. The author's aim is to find, especially in the story of the Patriarchs, justification for the laws and customs of his times. Caves I, II and IV have produced fragments of about ten manuscripts of this work. Its Hebrew style flows easily, and the text corresponds closely to that of the archetype presupposed by the (complete) Ethiopic and (incomplete) Latin versions. The insistence on a special form of solar calendar and on fixed dates for the main festivals—both important characteristics of the Qumrân sect (see below)—suggest that, in this case, the work was itself written by a member of the sect;[2] historical allusions make it probable that its composition occurred well before 100 B.C.

---

[1] Cf. *RB* LXIII, 1956, pp. 54 and 572.

[2] We should, however, be careful not to assume Essene authorship for any non-biblical work merely from the circumstance of its being found at Qumrân.

THE BOOK OF ENOCH

The pseudepigraphical Book of Enoch is likewise represented by ten or so fragmentary manuscripts from Cave IV. Hitherto we had known the work in an Ethiopic translation, some papyri from Egypt which gave sections of the Greek text, and some long quotations, especially in Syncellus. In the Ethiopic version the book consists of five sections and must be considered a compilation: chapters 1–36, Enoch's journey to other worlds; 37–71, apocalyptic 'Similitudes' on the Son of Man; 72–82, a reckoning of the movements of the sun and moon; 83–90, Enoch contemplates in a series of dream-visions the history of the world from the Creation until the times of the author, nations and individuals being symbolized by animals; 91–108, an Apocalypse of Weeks, followed by a parenetic section on the rich and poor, and an account of Noah's birth.

Five Aramaic manuscripts from Cave IV correspond partially to the first and fourth sections, i.e. Enoch's Journey and his Dream-visions; these sections, together with the last chapters of the book, must have once formed a separate work. The versions translated them more faithfully than they did the astronomical section.[1] The latter is represented by four Aramaic manuscripts from Cave IV, which provide a clearer and more intelligible text than that hitherto available. Of the last section the beginning has been preserved in one Cave IV manuscript. It too circulated as a separate work, as is also evident from a fragmentary Greek manuscript of the Byzantine period found among the Chester Beatty-Michigan papyri, which at the end bears the title of 'Epistle of Enoch'.

The absence of fragments from the second part, the 'Similitudes', is to be noted: it can scarcely be the work of chance. The 'Similitudes' are probably to be considered the work of a Jew or a Jewish Christian of the first or second century A.D., who reutilized the various early Enoch writings to gain acceptance for his own work and gave the whole composition its present form. The Enoch corpus is a sort of Pentateuch like the Torah, or Pentateuch of Moses, and the five books of Psalms, David's Pentateuch. The

---

[1] In *RB* LXV, 1958, pp. 71, 76 f., I have published two fragments from the Journeys, and a third from the astronomical section.

oldest parts of the corpus, or at least the fourth part, seem to have been composed after the death of Judas Maccabaeus in 160 B.C., as he is the latest historical figure to be alluded to in this section (ch. 90, cf. Charles' edition). The late redactor copied the Journey, the Visions and the Apocalypse of Weeks as he found them, but the astronomical treatise, which was of less interest to him, he condensed in a way that leaves it scarcely intelligible. His purpose was to set forth his speculations on the Son of Man, and to clothe them with the renowned patriarch's authority.

THE TESTAMENTS OF THE TWELVE PATRIARCHS

When the first discoveries were made at Qumrân, several scholars suggested, on the basis of internal criteria, that the pseudepigraphical *Testaments of the Twelve Patriarchs* were also remains of Essene literature. Actually, no trace has been found at Qumrân of the Hebrew or Aramaic archetype which some scholars have assumed to be the basis for our present Greek text. We have, however, been able to identify some of the sources used. A fragment from Cave I and some more important pieces from Cave IV belong to an Aramaic *Testament of Levi*, with a text far longer than that of the Greek text in the *Testaments of the Twelve Patriarchs,* but identical with that of Aramaic fragments recovered half a century ago from the Cairo Geniza. There is, moreover, a Greek manuscript of the *Testaments* from the tenth century in the library of Mount Athos, which contains two long additions to the *Testament of Levi*, a prayer of Jacob and some sacrificial prescriptions. The Aramaic of both these long additions has been found at Qumrân (fragments from Cave IV) and the second of them corresponds also to the Geniza manuscript.[1]

Recently we have identified a second *Testament*, that of Naphtali, written in Hebrew. The first fragment contains the genealogy of Bilhah, and once again its text is longer than that of the corresponding section of the Greek *Testament* (1.6–12). Later sections of the work contain considerations on the end of days—a theme scarcely mentioned in the corresponding Greek *Testament*.

Accordingly, we would be willing to ascribe to the *Testaments of the Twelve Patriarchs* an origin analogous to that of the Book of Enoch. A Jew or Jewish-Christian of the first or second century, using and adapting such Testaments as were already in circulation would have completed an analogous set of Testaments for all the Twelve Patriarchs. That these, as we have them, all came from one author can be seen from the repetition in each of the same literary form. Each consists of a pseudo-historical introduction, a parenetic section and a messianic and apocalyptic conclusion; and it is the second section, with its developments on virtues and vices, which is particularly dear to our author's heart; in it he gives a treatise on moral theology that is very revealing for the ethics of the circle in which he lived. Doctrinally important is the theme of the two Messiahs, who, for our author, seem already to be merged into only one person.[1] Other elements bear a Christian stamp, and since they cannot easily be considered as interpolations, they suggest a Christian rather than a Jewish origin for the *Testaments of the Twelve Patriarchs*.

OTHER OLD TESTAMENT PSEUDEPIGRAPHA

We have already alluded to a scroll from Cave I which was the last to be unrolled.[2] Written in Aramaic, this work is a collection of pseudepigraphical material concerning the Patriarchs arranged in a chronological order. The beginning of the scroll is missing: the partially preserved second column contains a section where Lamech is the narrator; in it he describes the miraculous birth of Noah—a theme which appealed also to the authors of Enoch 106, of another manuscript from Cave I (see *Discoveries* . . . I, pp. 84 ff.) and of fragments from the fourth cave, one of which even gives the baby's weight.

A new section starts with a quotation of Gen. 6.9; the account is put in the mouth of the patriarch Noah, who modestly adds: 'During all my days I have spoken the truth.' The section deals with the flood and subsequent happenings to the sons of Noah. The division of the earth among the sons of Noah is given in some detail and this description of the current Jewish concept of

---

[1] Cf. G. R. Beasley-Murray, *The Journal of Theological Studies* XLVIII, 1947, pp. 1–17.

[2] Only part of this work has so far been published, in *A Genesis Apocryphon, A Scroll from the Wilderness of Judaea*, Jerusalem 1956 (in Hebrew and English) by N. Avigad and Y. Yadin. The editors give a summary of the scroll's contents in so far as it has been deciphered, and Columns II and XIX–XXII in facsimile, transcription and translation.

the *Oikoumenê* will illuminate several passages in the corresponding section of Jubilees, 8 f.

The third part so far known deals with Abraham. It follows fairly closely the corresponding text of Genesis—most of the expansions here betray the writer's apologetic preoccupations.[1] The account of the expedition of the four kings is almost a verbatim translation (Targum) of Gen. 14, except that the place-names that occur in it are identified with sites known in the author's time.[2]

Other apocrypha from Qumrân deserve mention: a pseudo-Jeremianic work, conserved in several manuscripts, which, however, has only loose connexions with the rest of the known literature that is attributed to the Prophet or his secretary Baruch; the *Psalms of Joshua*, a work especially interesting in that it provides the fourth quotation in the *Testimonia*, a document we shall discuss in Chapter IV; and a *Vision of Amram*, the father of Moses and Aaron, an Aramaic apocryphon concerning the priestly family.[3]

From Cave IV comes the beginning of a small Aramaic scroll entitled *The Prayer of Nabonidus* (Plate 8). Its text runs as follows: 'The words of the prayer made by Nabonidus, king of (Assyria and of Ba)bylon, (the great) king, (when he was smitten) with a malignant disease, by the decree of the (Most High God, in the town of) Teima. "I was smitten (with a malignant disease) for a period of seven years, and became unlike (men. But when I had confessed my sins) and faults, God vouchsafed me a magician. He was a Jew from among (those exiled in Babylon). He gave his explanation, and wrote an order that honour and (great glory) should be given to the Name of the (Most High God. And thus

[1] E.g. he explains away the lie told about Sarah's identity (Gen. 12.13, cf. 20.2); he harmonizes Abraham's stay at Zoan with the date given in Num. 12.22; and he makes the Patriarch carry out the command of Gen. 13.17, after having contemplated the Promised Land (which, in the scroll, he does from the summit of Mount Haṣôr, the modern Jebel el 'Aṣûr, the highest point in central Palestine).

[2] Especially important is the identification of the vale of Shave 'which is the valley of the king' (Gen. 14.17) with the *plain of Bet-Karma*; this taken with the evidence in Josephus, St Jerome and the Talmud, seems to confirm Aharoni's suggestion that Ramat Raḥel (nearly three miles south of Jerusalem) is the site of the biblical Bet-Hakkerem. Cf. *Israel Exploration Journal* VI, 1956, pp. 102–11, 137–57.

[3] *RB* LXIII, 1956, p. 65 and, for the *Vision of Amram*, J. Starcky, orally.

he wrote: While) you were smitten with a (malignant) disease
(in the town of) Teima (by decree of the Most High God), you
prayed for seven years (to gods) of silver and gold, (of bronze,
iron), wood, stone and clay . . ." '

This account, which contains certain historical elements (Nabonidus, the last neo-Babylonian king and his stay of approxi-
mately seven years in the oasis of Teima) seems to be the source
used, either in an oral or a written form, by the author of the book
of Daniel when he is writing of Nebuchadnezzar's illness. Beneath his pen the name of the great king displaces that of Nabonidus, Teima is replaced by the more illustrious Babylon, and the
illness, although still lasting seven years, acquires features unknown to medical science.[1]

SECTARIAN LITERATURE: THE RULE OF THE COMMUNITY

The *Rule of the Community* (1Q S, called by its first editors 'The
Manual of Discipline') is known in a virtually complete manuscript from Cave I (Plate 15) and in ten fragmentary manuscripts
from Cave IV. The latter seem to preserve a purer text than that
of 1Q S, a copy whose errors and glosses make it sometimes
unintelligible. When the Cave IV texts are published, we shall be
able to reach a form of text closer to the original as it came from
the pen of its author (possibly the Teacher of Righteousness
himself).[2] After the title and introduction comes a liturgy for the
ceremony of Renewal of the Covenant (1Q S I.7–III.12). The
second part is doctrinal and discusses the Two Spirits (III.13–
IV.26). The third contains regulations (VI.1–IX.11) and especially
the community's penal code (VI.24–VII.25), while the last section
includes considerations on the appointed times and seasons, a
negative confession by the author and a hymn showing deep
spiritual feeling (IX.12–XI.22).

The roll of 1Q S had two appendices, the *Rule of the Congregation*
and a collection of *Benedictions* (*Discoveries* . . . I, pp. 107–30).
The first opens this way: 'This is the rule for the whole congrega-

---

[1] Cf. *RB* LXIII, 1956, pp. 407–15; Vogt, *Biblica* XXXVII, 1956, pp.
532 ff.; and for the connexion of this text with the 'Mene, Mene, Tekel
Upharsin' prophecy, D. N. Freedman, *BASOR* 145, Feb. 1957, pp. 31 f.

[2] Some differences in the form of the text, as our oldest manuscript from
Cave IV presents it, will be discussed in our treatment of the history of the
sect.

tion of Israel in the end of days.' It deals with their own community as they knew it, but from an eschatological viewpoint. It closes with a short description of the eschatological banquet over which the two Messiahs will preside. The second appendix exists in a very fragmentary condition, but originally it ran to at least six columns. In it are found Benedictions for the laity of the Community, for the Chief Priest (?), for the Priests, and for the Prince of the Congregation. The work is a literary compilation, rather than a ritual that was ever actually in use.

THE DAMASCUS DOCUMENT

After the *Rule of the Community*, the most important of the strictly sectarian works is the *Damascus Document*. This text had been known for fifty years, ever since two manuscripts of it (*A* and *B*) representing two distinct recensions of the work were discovered in Cairo and published by S. Schechter.[1] On the date of its composition and the milieu from which it came widely divergent hypotheses were put forward, oscillating from the pre-Maccabean period to that of the Qaraites well within the Middle Ages. Hardly any scholars then suspected that it was of Essene origin;[2] this has, however, now become certain since the discovery of the *Rule of the Community*, and especially since the identification of copies of the *Damascus Document* itself in Caves IV, V and VI. The text that the Qumrân exemplars present is substantially that of the *A* recension found in Cairo, but with some noteworthy additions. One of them occurs before the passage which forms the beginning of the Cairo copy; and the end of the work, missing in Geniza manuscript, is preserved in two manuscripts from Cave IV. Many other passages of legal character are also only known from Qumrân fragments and supplement the Cairo recensions.[3]

As is known, the work consists of two parts: the first comments on God's saving plan in history (i-viii, xix-xx), while the second gives detailed rules for the lives of members of the New Covenant in their camps in the land of Damascus. The Qumrân manuscripts, the oldest of which should be dated between 75 and 50 B.C.,

---

[1]*Fragments of a Zadokite Work* (*Documents of Jewish Sectaries I*), Cambridge 1910.

[2]Only I. Levi (*REJ* LXIII, 1912, pp. 1–19) and E. Meyer (*Ursprung und Anfänge des Christentums*, II, 399) even considered the possibility of a connexion.

[3]See Additional Note 3.

give us these two parts in one continuous text. The difference in literary character between the two parts of the book is no argument for their existence as originally independent works; many other compositions of this time (e.g., *Test. Levi*) show an analogous mixture of *genres*. A manuscript from Cave IV will be discussed later which seems to combine sections from the *Manual of Discipline* and the *Damascus Document* into one work.

THE RULE FOR THE WAR; THE HYMNS

The *Rule for the Final War* (Plate 17) is one of the works which best express the mentality of the Essenes during the last phase of their occupation of Qumrân. Its first editor, Sukenik, called it 'The War of the Sons of Light against the Sons of Darkness', but the original title is given in the damaged first line of the work, *Lem(aśkil Serek) hammilḥamah*, 'For the Sage—the Rule for the War'. It was first edited by Sukenik and Avigad ('*Oṣar*, . . . pp. 16 ff.)[1] and was the object of a detailed commentary by General Y. Yadin, especially important for the understanding of the military aspects of the work. Even though incomplete, the manuscript preserves the major part of the work. Fragments of three different manuscripts from Cave IV seem to follow the same text, but two other manuscripts from the same cave, one of them fairly well represented, attest the existence of a different recension.[2] Significantly enough the differences bear more on the hymnic sections of the work and less on the descriptive part. The following hypothesis may perhaps account for the origin and form of the work. As Yadin suggest, the descriptive portions of the work presuppose the existence of a military manual heavily indebted to Roman treatises *De re militari*; since striking parallels in organization are to be found between the apocalyptic army of our scrolls and Herod's forces, it is only natural to suppose that the philo-Roman Herod had such a manual adapted for the use of his own troops. This strictly military manual was probably adapted into a priest's *vade mecum* for the Holy War, and the latter work was variously expanded, especially in the hymnic sections. Its

---

[1] A few isolated fragments published in *Discoveries* . . . I, p. 135, and some of the unplaced fragments in '*Oṣar*, p. 47, have been fitted into their original places in the scroll by the writer (*RB* LXII, 1955, p. 198).

[2] C. H. Hunzinger, *ZAW* LXIX, 1957, pp. 131 ff.

date, accordingly, must be post-Herodian, and, indeed, palaeo-graphically all the six manuscripts so far known are from the first century A.D. The chief features of this work will be considered in our discussion of the sect's doctrines.

A long roll from Cave I, unfortunately badly damaged, presents us with a collection of hymns, most of which begin, 'I thank thee, O Lord, that . . .' (Plate 16). These *Thanksgiving Hymns* (in Hebrew, *Hodayot,* whence the abbreviation 1Q H) could well be at least in part the work of the Teacher of Righteousness himself, or else derived from his oral catechesis. This is suggested by the quality of their inspiration and by the high conception that the author has of the relation between God and man. One looks in vain for similar tones in the rest of contemporary literature. The first edition left a good number of fragments unplaced, but six fragmentary manuscripts from Cave IV promise to be of help in restoring parts of the original text. In chapters III and IV we shall give a few passages from these hymns.

COMMENTARIES ON BIBLICAL BOOKS

The biblical Commentaries of the Essenes have a uniform pattern. The biblical text is transcribed and then commented upon, verse by verse, the comment being introduced by a formula such as 'The explanation (*pešer*) of this is . . .', or 'The explanation of this word is . . .'. Hence we call them *pešārîm*, i.e. 'explanations'.

They follow certain rules of interpretation, which are partly arbitrary; there is speculation on a passage without reference to its context, explanation based on homonymy or simple assonance, separation of words belonging together in the text, metathesis, etc. We may distinguish between three types of Essene exegesis: in the first, the text is explained in relation to the sect's own history (e.g. the *pešārîm* of Habakkuk, Micah and Psalms); in the second, the explanation again concerns the sect, but in its relation with some ethnic groups in Palestine and its part in contemporary events (e.g. the Nahum *pešer*); and in the third the prophet's words are interpreted eschatologically (so in the *pešārîm* on Isaiah). The latter is often an explanation which respects more the intent of the inspired writer. However, these types are not kept rigidly separated, even though one of them usually predominates in a given commentary.

Closely related to this literary genre are the *Testimonia* which we shall discuss later, and also a commentary of messianic character on a *florilegium* of biblical texts. These documents contain quotations and short explanations of passages from Exodus, II Samuel, Isaiah, Psalms, Amos and Daniel. The texts are often quoted with the formula, 'As is written in the book of the prophet Isaiah, Daniel', etc. We should note that all manuscripts that contain *pešer*-type material come from the later period of the Qumrân community, and no one work seems to have existed in more than one copy. These isolated examplars would then be ephemeral compositions preserved in the author's own copy and are to be connected with the exposition of the Bible that were given in the sect's meetings for worship.

OTHER WRITINGS FOUND AT QUMRÂN

Many fragments from Cave IV contain hymnical material or else have a liturgical or sapiential character; these too, when they have been studied in detail, will provide us with many further details about the Essenes. In addition to the *Damascus Document* and the *Serek Hayyaḥad*, further samples of the sectarian Halakah ('Rules of Conduct') have been found in Cave IV, in which their laws and rites are justified by reference to texts from the Pentateuch. In their Halakah the Essenes are obsessed with questions of ritual purity even more than the Pharisees of the New Testament seem to have been.

We group together a series of manuscripts under the name of *Mišmarôt* or 'Courses', in which the rota of the priestly families' service in the temple is given in detail according to the solar calendar, and also synchronized with the lunar calendar. We shall cite some examples of these texts in chapter IV when we discuss the Qumrân calendar. Here we should observe that the 'monks' of Qumrân, although they had broken off relations with the Jerusalem priesthood, did not cease to ascribe an eternal value to the divine service of the priests and were convinced that it would be restored in the fullness of the Last Days.

Accordingly it is especially for the service of the temple in eschatological times that the duties of the priestly families are laid down. Indeed, there is an Aramaic work, which can be entitled *A Description of the Heavenly Jerusalem*, which contains an exceedingly detailed vision of the Holy City and Temple. It is obviously inspired by the last chapters of the book of Ezekiel. Fragments of it have been found in Caves I, IV, V and XI. Some fragments of a ritual in Aramaic from Cave II could belong to the same work.[1]

Horoscopes belong to a literary genre well known from the Babylonian tablets onwards. Two fragmentary columns from Cave IV give the signs of the Zodiac distributed over the days of the month. 'On the 13th and 14th (of the month of Tebet)', we read, 'Cancer . . .' Then follow predictions that can be drawn from thunder. 'If it thunders in the sign of the Twins, terror and distress caused by foreigners and by . . .'

This type of composition (*Brontologion*) is well attested in antiquity; the specimen closest to our Qumrân exemplar is a Greek Brontologion ascribed to Zoroaster (*Geoponica* I. 10). Its type survives to the present day; a list distributing the signs of the Zodiac over the days of the month in exactly the same way can be found in a modern Greek manuscript partially published in *Byzantinische Zeitschrift* XIV, 1905, p. 614.

Lastly a word should be said about the copper rolls that were discovered in the débris of Cave III. The text consists of twelve columns engraved on three sheets of metal that were originally riveted together. The whole roll is 2.4 metres long. It contains a list of about 60 deposits of treasure, hidden in various sites scattered over the Palestinian countryside, but mainly concentrated in the region of Jerusalem, near the Temple and in the cemetery of the Kedron valley. The total of gold and silver said to be buried exceeds 6,000 talents, or 200 tons—a figure that obviously exceeds the resources of private persons or of small communities.

In addition to these quantities of gold and silver, the roll mentions incense and precious substances which are said to be stored in vessels also made of valuable materials. The last ends with a description of a second hiding place where another copy of this catalogue is buried. All these motifs recur in other folkloristic works that give clues to buried treasure. An example of such folklore is found in Egyptian Arabic literature, the *Book of Buried Pearls and Hidden Treasures*, which Ahmed Bey Kamil

[1] M. Baillet, *RB* LXII, 1955, pp. 222-45.

published in Cairo in 1907. Here are two passages from the Qumrân copper roll:

'Near it (i.e. the preceding cache) beneath the southern corner of the portico in Zadok's tomb, beneath the pilaster of the exedra (a side-chamber of the tomb) there is a vessel of incense in pine wood and another in cassia wood'; and 'in the great cistern in the peristyle court, in a recess at the bottom, 900 talents are hidden in a hole opposite the upper opening.'

Here our rapid presentation of the most important manuscripts from Qumrân must end.[1] There are others which are still being studied and which deserve mention, but our readers will already realize the exceptional wealth of this library. It becomes even more striking if we remember that none of the religious groups of antiquity have given us information on their beliefs and way of life in a way comparable to that which the Essenes chose, when they bequeathed to us the books of their chief monastery.

[1]We have given a preliminary report of the non-biblical manuscripts of Cave IV in conjunction with J. M. Allegro, J. Strugnell, J. Starcky and C. H. Hunzinger in *RB* LXIII, 1956, pp. 60–67. For the other Qumrân caves, cf. Baillet and Milik, *ibid*, pp. 54–56. See also *VT* Suppl. IV, 1957, pp. 17–26.

III

HISTORY OF THE ESSENES

THIS chapter falls into two parts. We will first cite a passage found in Pliny, crucial for the interpretation of the archaeological evidence, and summarize the results of the excavations of the Qumrân region, adding a discussion of such Qumrân texts as are relevant to the sect's history. In the second part, we shall attempt to synthesize this material, together with the data to be found in classical writers, in a picture of the history of the Essene movement and of the Qumrân settlement.

A TEXT FROM PLINY

Pliny the Elder, the well-known author of the *Historia Naturalis*, has left us a useful description of Palestine, a country which he may have visited while he was travelling in the east. After mentioning the Dead Sea and its eastern shore, he comes to the Essenes who lived on the west coast (V. 17, 73): 'On the west coast of Lake Asphaltitis, (i.e. the Dead Sea) are settled the Essenes, at some distance from the noisome odours that are experienced on the shore itself. They are a lonely people, the most extraordinary in the world, who live without women, without love, without money, with the palm trees for their only companions. But they maintain their numbers, for recruits come to them in abundance, men who are wearied of life or driven by the changes of fortune to adopt their way of living. And so, through countless ages, hard though it is to believe, this people among which no children are born has survived. Others who feel repentance for their lives become their children. Lower down than the Essenes (*infra hos*) was the town of Engada ('Ain Gedi) which in the fertility of its soil and its palm groves was surpassed only by Jericho,[1] but which today is reduced like it (Jericho)

---

[1] The manuscripts read 'Jerusalem'; this is obviously a scribal error, since the reference to palm-groves can only apply to Jericho.

to a heap of ashes. Then comes the fortress of Masada in the mountains, it too at some distance from Lake Asphaltitis.'

It can easily be seen from the end of Pliny's account that he is alluding to the condition of Palestine after the First Jewish Revolt; but the Essene settlement at Qumrân, as the excavations show, was destroyed during this revolt. Such a mixing of contemporary information with anachronistic details is not unique in Pliny; in his account of Palmyra too he uses earlier geographic material.[1] Broadly speaking, the details provided by Pliny about the Essenes correspond to those of Josephus and Philo, which we shall discuss later. The latter writers, however, describe mainly the Essene communities scattered in the towns and villages of Palestine; Pliny alone mentions that there was a particularly important settlement west of the Dead Sea, at some distance from the shore and north of 'Ain Gedi. It has been noticed that in Pliny the preposition *infra* always means 'down-stream', and that, for the classical writers as well as for the authors of the Talmud,[2] the Dead Sea is a continuation of the Jordan; accordingly, 'Ain Gedi was 'down-stream' from the Essenes' site. Before the discoveries at Qumrân scholars had not paid sufficient attention to the precise meaning of the phrase *infra hos,* and used to place the Essenes' settlement in the vicinity of 'Ain Gedi. The ruins of Qumrân are virtually the only remains of any importance on the Dead Sea shore between 'Ain Gedi and Jericho. They also agree with his remark in being set back about half a mile from the shore itself, on a small plateau swept every afternoon by a cooling breeze.

THE EXPLORATION OF QUMRÂN

These ruins, however, received scarcely any attention from scholars. In the last century the explorer E. de Saulcy gave a brief description of them, but thought they were the remains of the biblical Gomorrah (since the local Arabs pronounce *q* as *g* Qumrân is heard as Gumrân). C. Clermont-Ganneau studied

---

[1] Cf. H. Seyrig, *Antiquités Syriennes,* III, 1946, p. 115, and J. Starcky, *Palmyre* (Paris 1952), p. 32.

[2] 'Its valley (i.e. that of Judaea) goes from 'Ain Gedi to Jericho' (*j.šebi'it* IX, 2).

them more closely and even excavated a few tombs with an unusual orientation, without reaching any conclusions. In this century G. Dalman recognized a Roman fort, and in this he was not completely mistaken. Independently, the same idea occurred to Féderlin who also found a reference in the Byzantine period to a farm at 'Ain Fešḫa, that depended on the monastery of Castellion at Ḫirbet Mird.[1] F. M. Abel in the early days of his scientific activity visited the ruins and suggested that the tombs belonged to a cemetery of an early Moslem sect.[2]

The first short season of excavations, which took place in December 1951 under the direction of Father R. de Vaux, O.P., and G. L. Harding, showed clearly a connexion between the former inhabitants of Ḫirbet Qumrân and the owners of the Cave I manuscripts. The pottery from both sites was of the same type and date. Furthermore, coins of the Roman Procurators provided data useful in determining at what period the site had been inhabited.

Between 1953 and 1956 there took place four further campaigns in which the archaeologists uncovered the whole extent of the ruins, and started to work on another Essene complex of buildings that lay farther south near 'Ain Fešḫa.[3] The results achieved by the archaeologists, combined with further study of the manuscripts, soon compelled scholars to conclude that it was the Essenes who were the principal occupants of the site and that the scrolls discovered had once formed part of their library.

DESCRIPTION OF THE RUINS

To reach Ḫirbet Qumrân today, the traveller leaves the Jerusalem–Jericho road when it comes out into the Jordan Valley and takes a macadamized road south-east to the north end of the Dead Sea. He then follows a rough track which climbs in and out of the wadis along the north-west coast of the Dead Sea

---

[1] *La Terre Sainte, Revue Illustrée de l'Orient Chrétien* XX, Paris 1903, pp. 209, 218, 232; cf. John Moschus, *Pratum Spirituale* 158 (Migne, *Patrologia Graeca* LXXXVII, 3026).

[2] For more details on early visitors to the site, cf. R. de Vaux, *RB* LX, 1953, pp. 83 f.

[3] Excavations at 'Ain Fešḫa were resumed in January 1958. See Additional Note 3.

for some four miles. On reaching the bed of the desolate Wadi Qumrân he can see ruins on the southern edge of a marly plateau about half a mile inland. Nineteen centuries ago a candidate for membership in the Essene sect would have followed a slightly different route from Jerusalem. The road to Jericho then emerged into the Jordan valley on the south side of the barren Wadi el-Qelt. From there a track wound along the foot of the Judaean mountains for some eight miles until it reached the Wadi Qumrân. As the would-be Essene skirted the foot of the marl terrace, he would have seen a path climbing steeply on to the plateau. This was practically the only means of approach whether one came by donkey, by cart or on foot, and it is still used today.[1]

The cemetery and ruins of Qumrân stand on a projecting spur of the marl terrace which is surrounded by precipitous ravines and joined to the rest only by a narrow neck to the west. A path leads up on to this spur and, before reaching the settlement itself, passes through a cemetery; this stops some four metres short of a sturdy wall running along the whole east side of the buildings. The living were thus kept free from contact with the dead. The main part of the cemetery numbers about 1,100 tombs dug in orderly rows and nearly all oriented north-south. They are covered by large stones and the burial is at a depth of more than one metre. The body lies in a loculus dug into the east wall of the tomb, protected from the earth above by flat stones or bricks. The head lies to the south and the hands are folded above the pelvis. In contrast with the Jewish practice of the period, no vases, jewels or coins are buried in the tomb, except for a few modest trinkets in the rare graves of women. Two smaller, perhaps later, cemeteries have been found at some distance to the north and south of the settlement.

---

[1] As one climbs today up the course of the Wadi Qumrân into the Buqei'a, one can see several places where steps have been cut and the surface levelled to make the path up easier. This route was certainly an important link in the eight and seventh centuries B.C. between 'Îr Hammelaḥ, (the Iron Age village at Qumrân) and three contemporary villages in the Buqei'a. This path, together with another one which comes down above Ras Feshḥa, must also have had some strategic importance for the Roman garrison at Qumrân at the end of the first century A.D. They would be useful for observing the movements of nomadic raiders moving into the region from the south and west. But its importance for the Essenes is not apparent.

Even from a distance, the general plan of the buildings, which cover in all an area 80 × 80 metres, is quite clear. They form a rectangular enclosure, with an impressive tower at the north-west, and behind it to the west lie some less imposing installations. The main entrance pierces a wall running out of the north of the tower. As one passes through this gate, the most noticeable feature is a solidly built canal supplied by an aqueduct leading from a small dam at the foot of a waterfall in the Wadi Qumrân. This canal brings water to seven large cisterns, scattered all over the settlement. The first cistern to which the canal comes is circular, but all the others are rectangular, with steps inside them enabling one to reach down to the level of the water in the dry season (Plate 12).

The western part of the settlement consists of various rooms used either as store rooms or as workshops: we find a cornmill, a baker's oven, other fires (for a forge?), silos for storing fruits, and rooms for storing grain. In the south-west corner of this part there is a stable with boxes for about eight pack-animals.

The entrance to the main building itself lies at the south-west corner of the tower. This tower had three floors, the third being built of bricks. A strong belt of stones was at one time put around the lower courses of the tower, and this narrows considerably the short corridor which leads from the entrance along the south of the tower into the centre of the main building. A small courtyard to the east of this corridor opens into two rooms, in the first of which a low plastered bench runs along the walls. A staircase from the courtyard leads up to an upper floor which ran above these two rooms and over a third long room to the east of them. Above this long room was a sort of verandah, well lit and aired. Here was the scriptorium which we have already described in chapter II. To the east of the tower there is the kitchen with well-preserved, rather rudimentary, fireplaces, and in the south-east corner of the main building are the laundry and sump for dirty water.[1]

The largest room of all lies outside on the south of the main block, 22 × 4.5 metres in size; its eastern end is covered by a roof supported by four central pillars (Plate 14). Here, doubtless, the liturgical gatherings of the Essenes were held: their reading

[1] So Couäsnon, orally, for De Vaux's earlier suggestion of a lavatory.

of and commenting on the Scriptures, and their prayers and sacred meals. In the south-west corner of this room over a hundred pieces of pottery were found, which had probably served for the last meals that the community took just before the monastery was destroyed. Near this there is a circular paved area of the floor; it is hard to see what this could have been except the base of a pulpit or lectern. An adjacent room served as a pantry, in which were found what had once been neat stacks of over a thousand pieces of pottery (Plate 10).

To the south-west there is a complete potter's shop, with the basin where the clay was kneaded, the tank in which it was kept, a hollow where the wheel once stood, and two conical kilns, one for baking jars, and the other for smaller pieces.

The region lying between the Ḥirbeh and Ras Fešḫa is watered by several springs and was cultivated in antiquity. Date palms especially were grown. In support of Pliny's reference cited above, many traces of beams of palm trees have been found in the construction of the buildings; moreover, date stones are often found in the caves. It would have been difficult to grow enough corn in these small oases for a large community; nor is there any conclusive evidence that it was grown in the Buqei'a. The Essene community must have relied on stores brought up from Jericho or sent by their benefactors; perhaps the pack-animals were kept to haul such supplies to Qumrân.

In normal times these buildings did not house many occupants, and a good part of the community must have lived near by in huts and caves (cf. Map 2). About thirty caves in the limestone cliffs were occupied, as is shown by the evidence of the pottery and manuscripts found in them. Some others were even cut out of the marly slopes of the plateau itself.[1]

THE PHASES OF OCCUPATION AT QUMRÂN

We shall now distinguish the various phases of occupation of the Qumrân settlement and determine the character and extent of the buildings in each of these. In such a reconstruction a

---

[1]On the excavation of Ḥirbet Qumrân cf. R. de Vaux, *RB* LX, 1953, pp. 83–106; LXI, 1954, pp. 206–36; LXIII, 1956, pp. 533–77; and on the survey of the Qumrân area *idem*, *RB* LX, 1953, pp. 540–61.

certain element of hypothesis is inevitable, the evidence being often too scanty to permit a definite conclusion.[1]

When the Essenes first came to establish themselves on the shore of the Dead Sea, they did not choose a virgin site. A fragmentary ostracon, a royal seal stamped on a jar-handle and potsherds clearly indicate a previous occupation, dating from the eighth and seventh centuries B.C. (Iron II). The plan of the buildings of that time, somewhat obscured by later Essene constructions, can be restored by comparison with the three contemporary sites in the Buqei'a. It was a rectangular enclosure built of roughly dressed stones. Along the inside of one, two or four of these walls were small rooms, called by archaeologists 'casemates'. In such enclosures, or beside them, there is always to be found a large cistern and the entire complex lay close to a fertile bowl, about which large dams were built to retain the moisture. At Ḥirbet Qumrân itself the four walls of this old rectangle are easily identified, and to the west of it, perhaps in a walled annexe, there is a deep round cistern. To the south of Ḥirbet Qumrân, in the small plain near 'Ain Fešḫa, there is another Iron II enclosure, bigger than that of the Ḥirbeh but with rather flimsy walls. It may have been nothing more than a pen for flocks and herds. A very long retaining wall, running from north to south, built in exactly the same way as those of the Buqei'a, kept the cultivated fields to the east from being harmed either by violent mountain floods or by animals. From the detailed list of place names in Josh. 15, it is even possible to recover the Israelite names of these settlements. The district of 'the Desert' described in Josh. 15.61 contains six villages, Bet Ha 'arabah (near Jericho), 'Ain Gedi and four others between them. One of these is called 'Îr Hammelaḥ, i.e. the city of (the sea of) salt. Its identification with Qumrân, tentatively proposed even before the excavations, now becomes certain, especially since the three remaining names can be assigned to the three contemporary sites of the Buqei'a. In a recent study of the list of Judaean place names in Joshua, F. M. Cross and G. E. Wright have tried to put the origin of these villages as early as the reign

[1] In this we mainly follow the analysis of de Vaux, *locc. citt.* On certain points of difference he has clarified his position and criticized ours in *RB* LXIV 1957, pp. 635 f.

of Jehoshaphat (II Chron. 17.12). The pottery found in them, however, does not allow a date earlier than the eighth century, where an even better literary *rapprochement* can be made with the activity of King Uzziah, who 'constructed towers in the desert and dug many cisterns' (II Chron. 26.10).[1]

When the Essenes left Jerusalem to settle in the ruins of the City of Salt, they cleaned out the round cistern and built near by two other rectangular cisterns, all of which collected the rain water from the flat surface around. They built some modest rooms around these, perhaps cleared and re-utilized some of the Iron II casemates and installed a new potter's kiln inside the old enclosure. This is the excavators' phase Ia. It should be stressed that when the later large-scale installation was completed, most traces of the earlier occupation were obliterated; it is therefore understandable that hardly any datable small objects can be attributed to this phase. It is a datum of archaeological experience that the earliest phase of an occupation leaves virtually no objects. Even the sherds of such a period will be picked up and ground down to make new pots. However, a few silver coins of the Seleucid kings, dating from *c.* 130, and some of John Hyrcanus' bronze coinage, in all fifteen pieces, could have been lost during this period. Whether this phase lasted ten, twenty, or forty years, it is certain that at some time in Hyrcanus' reign (135–104 B.C.) the site entered into its most flourishing stage.

Here we get a complete change, a radical rebuilding. An impressive and well-planned structure of two and three floors fills in the older enclosure. The settlement expands beyond these walls to the west and south. The increased number of inhabitants could no longer rely on a haphazard supply of rainwater, and the extensive and complicated network of canals and cisterns was installed at this time. A dam was built to catch the water which, once or twice each spring, runs down the Wadi Qumrân. An aqueduct was cut out of the rock and a trench dug through the

[1] Cf. J. T. Milik and F. M. Cross, *RB* LXIII, 1956, pp. 74–76 and *BASOR* 142, April 1956, pp. 5–17; also F. M. Cross and G. E. Wright, *JBL* LXXV, 1956, p. 224. The identifications of the four sites depend partly on the fact that *no other* Iron II sites were found in the region; this argument gains force from my recent survey of the region to the east of Tekoa, which might have been reckoned in the desert district. Here too no Iron II villages were found.

marl to bring all this water to the settlement, where it was stored in cisterns. The whole system was carefully coated with impermeable plaster.[1] The fact that so large an area was built over, and the water storage capacity so enlarged, suggests that the occupants of the settlement had become far more numerous that they were in Phase Ia. Although the small group of inhabitants of the early years could have lived in economic isolation from the outside world, the enlarged community of Phase Ib could not. They were probably forced to rely on supplies of food, especially corn, brought in from outside; and this may account for the greater use of coins during this period.

The closing years of this phase were marked by two disasters, a fire, which ravaged the settlement from south to north, and an earthquake. The traces of both are very clear. Especially in the open areas to the north and north-west, there is a thick layer of ashes beneath the level of the Phase II reconstruction, showing the extent and violence of the fire. Even more impressive are the traces of the earthquake. The marl plateau was shaken and the eastern edge of it dropped about 50 centimetres. The fault runs through the whole length of the settlement, tearing apart cisterns and cracking the walls that lay in its path; those that supported more than one storey were left in an unsafe condition. It seems that we can date this destruction to 31 B.C., when Josephus records a great earthquake which caused widespread damage throughout Judaea and especially in the Jordan valley.[2] The archaeological evidence from Qumrân is not unambiguous as to the order of these two events. It is quite possible that when the roofs collapsed in the earthquake they accidentally caught fire, but there are few fireplaces in the settlement and in the daytime when Josephus tells us that the earthquake occurred, not even these would be lit. The thick layer of ashes suggests a very violent conflagration, better to be explained as the result of a conscious attempt to burn down the whole building; so the ashes may show the traces of an intentional destruction of Qumrân.

No major rebuilding of the damaged settlement took place for some years until the beginning of the reign of Archelaus in

---

[1]See Additional Note 4.
[2]*Ant.* XV.v, 121–47; *War* I.xix, 370–80.

4 B.C. Several indications of a long interval can be seen in the ruins of the settlement. Near the north-west corner of the western building there is a thick layer of ashes, the result of the fire mentioned above. On top of this there is a layer of mud which settled there because the aqueduct overflowed; this presupposes a period when the system of canals and cisterns was not being properly supervised. This layer had become 75 centimetres thick before it was put to use as the foundation for a new wall which reinforced this building. Again, during the work of reconstruction the collapsed buildings were thoroughly cleaned out and swept, and the débris was thrown away in a small ravine to the north of the settlement. In 1953 a large trench was dug into the slope of this ravine, which established that it was indeed a 'fill', and produced pottery, an inscribed ostracon, plaster and numerous coins: of these, all but one are of the Hasmonean kings or their contemporaries; there is no coin of Herod's reign, and only one from the reign of Archelaus, perhaps lost by one of those who filled the dump. It should be stressed that this dump was only used on one occasion, when the rebuilding was being started; no later coins were found in it, nor can any strata be detected in it such as would be expected were it in continuous use over a longer period.

That there was an interval before rebuilding is therefore certain on archaeological grounds, but the evidence is to our mind insufficient to demonstrate the excavators' further conclusion that the site ceased to be occupied during this period. An argument for this might be seen in the absence of Herodian pieces among the coins found in the rubble cleaned out of the building before its reconstruction. However, this argument is based on the coins found in one place alone, whereas those found in the whole settlement militate against the excavators' numismatic argument that the finding of only five bronze coins from Herod's reign suggest an abandonment during some part of that period. Rather, the series of bronze coins, which starts with Hyrcanus I, continues uninterruptedly until the First Jewish Revolt, and the proportional frequency of each issue corresponds to that of other contemporary sites and casual finds. As is usual, the coins of Jaanaeus (103–76 B.C.) and Agrippa I (A.D. 37–44) are the commonest; next come those of the procurators under Tiberius and

Nero; while pieces from the long reigns of Hyrcanus II (63–40 B.C.) and Herod the Great (37–4 B.C.) are relatively infrequent. Although the evidence is slight, it would seem more plausible to assume that a certain number of Essenes continued to live in the ruins in the interval before rebuilding; the rough huts that they would have built would leave almost no traces for an excavator to detect. Palaeography gives us a further indication of at least a diminution in Essene activity during this time. For manuscripts written in the so-called 'Herodian' script are proportionately less frequent than Hasmonean and post-Herodian ones.

The political situation in Palestine after the death of Herod enables us to understand why a new afflux to Qumrân should take place, thus necessitating the restoration of the damaged buildings. This major rebuilding (Phase II) followed fairly closely the lines of the old settlement. Because of a fear of damage from another earthquake, the upper parts of the structure were strengthened, belts of stone being put round the base of the north-west tower, the western building and the pantry. Some parts were abandoned, such as the cistern that had been split by the earthquake—a fact which might suggest a slightly reduced number of inhabitants. Although some new areas were enclosed (e.g. on the north side of the main building) the purpose of this was probably to reduce the number of secondary entrances and so increase the building's defensibility.

This second phase of Essene occupation lasted about seventy years. Its end came in the summer of A.D. 68, the third year of the First Jewish Revolt. Josephus tells us that the Legio X Fretensis and Legio XV Apollinaris compaigned in the Jordan valley, destroying the major defensive points.[1] At Qumrân seventy-three bronze coins of the year II of the First Jewish Revolt were found; the year III, starting in the spring of 68, furnished only five coins. Together with this Jewish revolutionary issue we find coins of the year 67–8 minted on the coast, nine from Caesarea and four from Dora. In these mints the Roman Emperors used to strike coins for the provinces and the legions, and it can be safely assumed that these pieces belonged to the pay of Roman legionaries. Traces of a violent fire and several arrow heads, with the

---

[1]*War* IV.VIII, 449 f.

three-winged form typical of the Roman army, show that some resistance was offered to them.[1]

After the destruction of the settlement a small garrison was left at Qumrân for some decades. They levelled the thick layer of fallen stones and beams and built a few modest barracks inside the ruins (Phase III). The main group of rooms of this period was found above the south-west corner of the central Essene building, where the scriptorium and council chamber had been. Here were found coins, the latest of them minted about A.D. 90. About that time this frontier post must have been abandoned. Some decades

[1]The stocks of broken pottery in the hall and pantry should also be considered as traces of the Roman attack. They were found shattered by the collapse of the roof, which fell during the fire that swept through the building. De Vaux, however, sees in the broken pottery in the pantry a trace of the earthquake and so distinguishes it from that found in the hall itself. Those who assign weight to palaeographical arguments should consider that one of the bowls in this pantry has a proper name scratched on it in a script typical of the first century of our era. This argument alone, based on five letters, would be insufficient. But a supporting stratigraphical point can be made. De Vaux (*RB* LXIII, 1956, p. 544; see his discussion of our position in *RB* LXIV, 1957, p. 635) distinguishes three phases. In the first the whole pantry was in use and this was destroyed by the earthquake of 31 which broke all the stacked pots. In the second only the front of the pantry was in use, the broken pottery being bricked up behind a small wall in the middle of the room. On the ruins of this phase, the Romans built some small rooms. As we remember, however, the three phases of this room's history must be traced in another way. Although the earthquake of 31 damaged the pantry, during the reconstruction the S.E. end of the room was strengthened by an additional outside wall, although on de Vaux's theory this was the unused part. The existence of a dividing wall in the middle of the room is not clear and, on the analogy of the method employed in other parts of the settlement, we would expect broken pottery to be cleared out of the building before resettlement. The sherds which, according to de Vaux, were bricked in by the 'wall' were not merely found behind it, but also in front and even under it. In fact the few stones found are hardly sufficient to form a real wall. Once this 'wall' is disposed of, it is evident that the whole pantry was used up to the end of Phase II, at which time it was destroyed together with the rest of the settlement and later re-used by the Romans. De Vaux argues that the pottery of the pantry is typical of the first phase, but a close reading of his description shows that the only difference between these pots and those of Phase II lies in the form of the base of the bowls; this alone, however, is not a sufficient criterion. Identical and contemporary forms of pottery can have different bases; e.g. we find in the same period at Qumrân bowls with flat, concave and ring bases. To establish de Vaux's reconstruction there should be a clear difference in type between the pots from the pantry and those from the south-west corner of the assembly hall; as we remember the pieces, this difference cannot be detected.

later the buildings served as a refuge for the partisans of Bar
Kokhba, whose sojourn there is indicated by thirteen coins lost
there. In the following centuries dust covered the ruins more and
more, and only some transient monks and shepherds left traces
of their passage.

QUMRÂN AND THE ESSENES

We have just given a brief sketch of the archaeological remains
at Qumrân and their history. The main period of occupation is
clearly that which stretches from the end of the second century
B.C. to the first Jewish Revolt, Phase Ib being the most flourishing
of all. During this period of almost 200 years what was the pattern
of life followed by those living in and about Ḥirbet Qumrân?

The above account of the ruins makes it sufficiently clear to
the reader that we are not dealing with a Palestinian village of
the normal type, with separate dwellings for each family unit
but rather with a group of structures designed for occupation by
a community. To recapitulate, we have found a carefully planned
hydraulic system (with reservoirs, aqueducts and canals all linked
together, settling tanks, cisterns and communal basins); workshops for the production of the utensils and food necessary for a
community living mainly in economic isolation (i.e. pottery,
smithy, bakery, mill and food stores); rooms and equipment for
communal use (laundry, kitchens, refectory, assembly halls); and
lastly, a cemetery neatly and systematically arranged, to whose
traces of planning one can find no parallel in the other Jewish
cemeteries of the period.

Was the site inhabited by this community the same as that to
which Pliny referred when speaking of the Essenes? Yes, for the
details that he gives are true of the buildings at Qumrân, and, as
we observed above, no other important ruins have been found
between Jericho and 'Ain Gedi. This conclusion becomes in-
escapable, if one further compares the results of the excavations
with the data found in Philo and Josephus and with the information derived from the texts found in the adjacent caves.

THE EVIDENCE OF THE QUMRÂN TEXTS

We shall now discuss the evidence to be found in the Qumrân
texts that may be useful for the reconstruction of the sect's history. We will not make a systematic use of the information found

in Josephus and the Books of Maccabees until we come to our synthetic presentation of the sect's history, though we may have occasion to use them intermittently in this section. It is not to be expected that the events of importance to the sect will have received the same degree of attention from these authors. Sectarian events often escaped their notice, or else were described in a very different way; but when it comes to matters of political history, such as the death of rulers or the reconstruction of cities, we should be chary of postulating unrecorded events.

There is not a single historical work (in our sense of the word) in the Qumrân library. The absence of written chronicles shows that for knowledge of its history, the Qumrân sect depended uniquely on its oral tradition. Accordingly, in the latter days of the sect's existence a certain blur in the details of historical information can be expected. Being indifferent to a factual or objective presentation of the past, and living in intense eschatological expectation, the sectarians tended to confuse the historical and eschatological levels when they came, in the course of their religious writings, to refer to historical events. In interpreting these allusions to historical events, one cannot stress the use of tenses. The writer may use the past or the future, as he writes from the viewpoint of his own time or from that of the inspired author on whom he is commenting. In this section we shall study such historical references as exactly as possible and try to determine what events could provoke such allusions. However the absence of an Essene interest in history, in the modern academic sense of the word, means that a coherent picture of the vicissitudes of the Essene movement, such as we shall attempt in the next section, would be almost impossible if we were forced to rely on Essene documents alone.

Among the Qumrân texts which are richest in historical allusions two groups must be distinguished. First in reliability are those which are more or less contemporary with the events to which they refer. Here, too, we have to depend on hypothesis; not only must we detect datable events hypothetically, but also rely on hypothesis in the dating of the composition of the works in the Qumrân library. Palaeography however enables us to establish, at least within two generations, the time in which our earliest exemplar of a book was copied.

In the first category we place the *Damascus Document* and the *Psalms of Joshua*. The second group consists of the *pešārîm* or commentaries on the biblical books, all of them dating from the last phase of the Qumrân settlement. The date of composition of these texts can most probably be determined accurately; it seems that each of them existed only in one autograph copy and the date of the manuscript is therefore probably also the date of composition. In using this group of texts we must be more critical because of the length of time which separates them from the events they refer to, such as the founding of the sect. Allusions to the events of that time may be confused by reminiscences of later events, or new religious attitudes.

THE DAMASCUS DOCUMENT

As far as the *Damascus Document* is concerned, the oldest copy we have was written *c.* 75–50 B.C. It is a fairly extensively preserved manuscript, abbreviated provisionally 4Q D^b. It is significant to note that this work, in contrast with the *Manual of Discipline*, abounds with historical allusions.

The first historical reference is found at the beginning (I. 5–12):

> And in the epoch of Wrath, 390 years after he had given them into the hands of Nebuchadnezzar, King of Babylon, he visited them; and he caused to grow forth from Israel and Aaron a new planting, to inherit his land and to feast on the best fruits of his soil. And they understood their iniquities, and became conscious that they were guilty men; but they were like the blind and like them that grope for their way for twenty years. And God considered their works, how they sought him with a perfect heart, and he raised up for them a Teacher of Righteousness to direct them in the way of his heart and to make the last generations know what he would do to the last generation, the congregation of traitors.

The interval from the exile to this crucial period is not to be taken exactly. Information about the Persian period was rather vague among the Jews, and the number of years given is a symbolical one derived from Ezek. 4.5. In general terms, however, we are near Maccabean times. Before the Teacher of Righteousness himself appeared on the scene, another important event took place, the crystallization of a group of laymen and priests (Israel and Aaron) which, whatever the political meaning of 'inherit his land' may be, was feeling its way towards a new cultic and moral programme. For about twenty years (this is scarcely a symbolic number) they were somewhat confused either in religious or political aims. This fairly-well defined group can be plausibly identified with the congregation of the Asidaeans mentioned in I Macc. 2.42:

> Then the congregation of the Asideans joined them (i.e. Mattathias Maccabaeus and his friends). These were men of valour from Israel, everyone a volunteer for the Law.

It is clear that this group existed before Mattathias raised the revolt in 167 B.C. Their warlike but chiefly religious aims are clear, and one of the phrases used of them, 'a volunteer for the Law', occurs several times in Essene texts in descriptions of members of their community. Allowing for their existence for a certain number of years before 167 B.C., the period of twenty years preceding the appearance of the Teacher of Righteousness will take us well into the reign of Jonathan (160–43).

In the *Damascus Document* there does not seem to be any clear allusion to the period of the Teacher's activity nor to the precise nature of the circumstances which led his followers to break off from the rest of the Jewish people and to form a separate congregation. For the author the centre of interest seems to lie in other events. But at the end of the passage cited there is an allusion to the congregation of traitors. This group is described in the following lines (I. 13–21), where we should note especially the phrase, 'those who seek after smooth things', as it will recur in the later *pešārîm*. From the general description of this group it is clear that the differences between them and the sect are purely religious, dealing with interpretation of biblical laws (*Halakah*). As leader or contemporary of this 'congregation of traitors' we find a figure variously described as 'the scornful one', and 'he who drips (i.e. preaches) to Israel waters of falsehood'. It should be noticed that this opponent is, however, not merely a religious figure, but something more. From the expression, 'what he would do to the last generation', it is clear that in this section the author of the *Damascus Document* is describing his own times.

. Two other passages should be cited which relate to these 'last' times':

> And from the day when the Teacher of the community died until the extermination of all the men of war who were followers of the Man of Lies (there will be) about forty years (XX. 13 ff.).[1]
>
> From the day when the Teacher of the community died until the rising of a Messiah from Aaron and Israel (XIX. 35–XX. 1).

The 'rising of a Messiah' is a strictly eschatological event which certainly has not yet come. In the first quotation the terminus is probably also in the future. The analogy is from Israel's desert wanderings; for forty years had to pass, and all the generation that had been in Egypt had to die, before Israel could enter the Promised Land. It is clear that the book is written at some time during this struggle with the Man of Lies which takes place after the death of the Teacher and which is the centre of the author's interest. Whatever the eschatological interpretation of this period, we should notice the warlike characteristics of the Man of Lies, who can only be the contemporary secular head of the Jewish people. In CD XX. 15, where we find a continuation of the prediction of the forty year period, the writer expresses disapproval of this leader.

> And in that period the wrath of God will be kindled against Israel, as he has said, 'There will be no prince, and no ruler, and no judge and none to reprove in righteousness.'

The third group of historical allusions relates to an exodus to the 'Land of Damascus'. These we shall discuss later; here it is sufficient to note that they are found in the context of the persecutions that beset the sect under the 'Man of Lies'.

---

[1]As mentioned above, there is no evidence from Cave IV that the sect knew the B recension of the *Damascus Document* from which this quotation comes. But it is certain that the manuscript A, with whose recension the Cave IV manuscripts agree, does not give us the end of the first part of the work. A few fragments of the 4Q manuscripts belong to this lost part, and contain a text substantially the same as that in the B recension.

4Q TESTIMONIA

Another early historical allusion is found in the last quotation of *4Q Testimonia*. This document itself was written about 100–75 B.C. and the work, the *Psalms of Joshua*, from which the quotation is taken must have been composed at least some decades before this. Although it is difficult to determine the precise nature of this work, it seems to be a tendentious writing which draws a picture of Joshua the charismatic leader who led the Israelites in their conquest of the promised land. He was recalled for the sake of contrast with the contemporary military and political figures; one immediately thinks of such usurping *conquistadores* as Jonathan and Simon. If it deals with sectarian history, as it must, it will be almost contemporary with the events to which it alludes. The passage cited from this work opens with Joshua's curse on Jericho and whoever should rebuild it (Josh. 6.26). After a small blank space in the manuscript there follows what seems to be an explanation of this biblical passage, a description of circumstances which seemed to the commentator to have called this curse into effect.

At the time when Joshua finished praising and giving thanks in his praises, he said: '*Cursed be the man who will build this city; with his first born he will lay its foundation and with his last born he will set up its gates*. And behold, cursed be the man of Belial who stands forth to be a fowl[er's sn]are for his people and destruction to all his neighbours. And he stood forth and [made his sons] rulers, and both of them became vessels of violence. And they built again this [city], and established for it a wall and towers to provide a refuge for wickedness [in the land and a thing of great shame] in Israel, a horrible portent in Ephraim and in Judah . . . and they wrought apostasy in the land and a thing of great shame among the sons of Jacob. [And they poured forth] blood like water on the ramparts of the daughter of Zion, and in the bounds of Jerusalem.'[1]

[1]*4Q Testimonia* was published by J. M. Allegro in *JBL* LXXV, 1956, pp. 182–7. The reconstruction given above is based on a combination of *4Q Testimonia* and *4Q Psalms of Joshua* which J. Strugnell has put at my disposal. Three technical explanations should be given: (1) The text reads

There can hardly be any doubt that the allusion here is to early Hasmonean rulers and their activity, not only in Israel, but also among the surrounding populations. The father has as his associates during his life or as his successors two sons who are called 'vessels of violence', an epithet applied by Jacob to his sons Levi and Simon (Gen. 49.5). The sentence which follows, where the rebuilding of 'this city' is mentioned, is better understood grammatically as an activity of the two sons and not of their father as well. As far as concerns the identification of 'this city', the biblical citation itself is inconclusive. In the book of Joshua it certainly refers to Jericho, but until we know more about the nature of the *Psalms of Joshua*, stress cannot be laid on this. As the citation stands, we have 'this city' instead of 'this city Jericho' which is found in the Masoretic text. But this is indecisive, as the quotation in several places follows the LXX text tradition, which also here omits 'Jericho'. We should in any case confine ourselves to the commentary and not to the biblical text. In this we find two details: the city is of central importance in the life of the people, and the consequence of the rebuilding of 'this city' is bloodshed in Zion and Jerusalem. It is hard to accept that the text should refer to Jericho and to historically unattested building operations there.

We should, therefore, look for a situation where Jerusalem was rebuilt, either by a father with his two sons or more probably by these two sons alone. For palaeographical reasons, we exclude the identification with Alexander Jannaeus and his sons Aristobulus and Hyrcanus II.[1] A reconstruction of Jerusalem could be

---

'*ḥd bly'l* 'a worthless fellow', but the '*yš* written over the line is certainly a correction for '*ḥd*. It is, indeed, not placed above the word it corrects but slightly to the right of it: this however occurs elsewhere. (2) The Hebrew word corresponding to 'made rulers', *whmšyl* or *wymšyl*, I consider after checking the original of 4*Q Testimonia* to be practically certain. The *m* is clearly followed by a *š*. In this context hardly any other word can be suggested. *bnyw*, 'his sons', is again fairly certain as it is presupposed by 'both of them' in the next phrase. (3) The reconstruction of the phrase 'a refuge for wickedness in the land, and a thing of great shame in Israel' was suggested to me by Strugnell. It is a plausible conjecture on the basis of the fragmentary text of 4*Q Psalms of Joshua*.

[1]This identification was proposed by Dupont-Sommer before the publication of 4*Q Testimonia* on the basis of the *Habakkuk Commentary*'s allusions to the building activities of the Wicked Priest.

attributed to one or other of his two sons, it is true. Aristobulus may have engaged in buildings activity in 65–63, as the city was twice besieged in that period. Hyrcanus received permission from Julius Caesar to rebuild the city, although it was actually Antipater who started the work in 47 B.C. (*Ant.* XIV. IX, 156). In neither of these cases, however, are both brothers involved. For when Aristobulus would have reconstructed, Hyrcanus was in exile; and by the time of Hyrcanus' rebuilding Aristobulus was dead.

It is not necessary to look for two sons, one of who was the firstborn and the other the last—so Dupont-Sommer and to some extent F. M. Cross. This detail is given only in the biblical citation and not in the commentary. To attach importance to it would be a mistake analogous to that of using the text of Habakkuk and not the *pešer* for the reconstruction of the sect's history.

As mentioned before, we believe that the commentary refers to Jerusalem and in this we agree with Dupont-Sommer. Cross, even if he does not exclude the Holy City, prefers to refer the event to Jericho, but since he grants the possibility of Jerusalem too, we shall not dispute this point further. Cross's identification of the three figures is the following: the father is Simon and his sons are Judas, probably the eldest, and Mattathias, the youngest. That Simon reconstructed Jerusalem, or rather finished Jonathan's reconstruction, is certain (I Macc. 13.10; 14.37) but there is no literary evidence for the association of his sons with him in this work. Again, it is true that Simon met his end with his two sons at Dok, but his two sons seem rather insignificant figures. Cross's main argument, that *all three* were killed, is irrelevant to a study of this document. The biblical text refers to the death of two sons by their father's hand as a 'foundation sacrifice', but the commentary interprets this as meaning that the father, through the agency of his two sons, would rebuild 'this city'.

If, however, we retain Simon as one of the two rebuilders and associate with him his brother Jonathan, who started the major reconstruction, have we then got a satisfactory identification for the two sons of the text? In this assumption the 'Man of Belial' has to be Mattathias Maccabaeus. Dupont-Sommer practically accuses us of blasphemy in proposing this slander against the 'heroic and holy priest who gave the signal for revolt against the impious invader, the father of the glorious hero of his nation's liberation'. This gallant reaction forgets the common historical phenomenon that a great man is not depicted by his supporters and his opponents in the same colours. Whatever may have been the attitude of the Asidaeans, *sensu stricto*, to Mattathias, once the Essenes broke away from one or more of his successors, they could easily include in their disapproval the ancestor of the ruling dynasty. This Semitic custom needs no comment. A favourite Arabic curse, *yiḥrib bet abuk* (*amwatak*), 'May God destroy your father's (ancestors') house,' implies no enmity towards anyone other than its immediate recipient.

Lastly, in the explanation of Joshua's curse one historical event is mentioned, the reconstruction of Jerusalem by two brothers. From Josephus and the Books of the Maccabees we know of only one such set of circumstances in that period to which archaeological and palaeographical evidence directs us: the activity of Jonathan and Simon between 152 and 142 B.C.

THE HABAKKUK COMMENTARY

Another important source of allusions to Essene history is the *Commentary on Habakkuk*. The palaeographical date of the Cave I manuscript is not quite obvious. On the whole, the script appears to be of the first half of the first century A.D. Although a few letters seem to argue for an earlier time, the dating of the manuscript depends upon the typologically later letter-forms which are in the majority.[1] The palaeo-Hebrew script used for copying the divine name is especially late and could not come from any part of the first century B.C. If this is so, the distance in time between the origins of the sect and the composition of this work, and the fact that the knowledge of sectarian history was handed down orally, should prepare us for some confusion in details.

From this book we will now cite the passages which seem to be more directly concerned with the history of the sect, its founders and its persecutors. Another group of comments in it relates to the Kittiim, about whose identity there was considerable discussion when the Qumrân documents were first discovered, some seeing in them the Seleucid empire and others the Roman.

[1] For this date, against other palaeographers, see now N. Avigad, *Scripta Hierosolymitana* IV, 1957, pp. 74–6.

A fragment of the *Commentary on Nahum*[1] resolves this question by the expression 'from Antiochus to the rising of the rulers of the Kittiim'. This can only mean: 'until the establishing of Roman authority (in the Middle East)', the rulers being the Roman governors of the province of Syria from 62 onwards. Exactly the same expression occurs in pHab IV. 5, and all other references to the Kittiim have therefore to be referred to the Romans. However, the apocalyptic Essene mind, especially when obliged to give a continuous exposition of a prophetic text, cannot be expected either to confine itself to the events of one period, or to separate out different events into clear groups. The similarly apocalyptic early Christians can find in the same section of the Bible allusions to the past, the present and the *eschaton*. We will, therefore, for the moment, leave on one side those passages referring to the Roman period and not directly to the sect's history at all, and deal first with those that allude to the circumstances surrounding the foundation and growth of the sect.

The passage pHab VIII. 8–13 reads:

> Its meaning concerns the Wicked Priest who at the beginning of his term of office (*'wmdw*) acted faithfully. But when he became governor (*mšl*) of Israel, his heart became proud, and he abandoned God and betrayed the commandments for the sake of wealth. And he plundered and took the wealth of violent men who rebelled against God, and he laid his hand upon the wealth of nations, and wrought sinful iniquity and followed the paths of abomination in utter impurity.

The situation referred to is one in which a ruler begins his period of office acceptably, but later forfeits the sect's esteem. The meaning of two important words in this section must be made clear: *'amad* and *mašal*. *'amad* is a general term which refers to the performance of any office, political, religious or eschatological. *mašal* can never be translated 'be king'—in this the usage at Qumrân is consistent; the Seleucid kings are always *malkê Yawan,* the Roman governors always *mošelê hakkittiim*. In our text, then, *mašal* cannot refer to a Jewish *king*. This gives us an important *terminus ante quem* for the setting of the text. The Wicked Priest

[1]Published by J. M. Allegro, *JBL* LXXV, 1956, pp. 89–93.

must be a predecessor of Aristobulus I (104–3) who first took the title of king. *Mašal* could refer, however, to the Greek title *meridarches* or *ethnarches*; such a dignity, together with the high priesthood, was borne by John Hyrcanus, Simon and Jonathan. Jonathan (160–42) was the leader of Israel without any official title for eight years. But in 152 he became High Priest at the nomination of Alexander Balas; in 150 he was nominated by the same emperor as military and civil governor of Judaea, and in 145 Antiochus VI made him governor of all Syria. His successors, Simon and Hyrcanus, were for the whole of their period of rule both High Priests and Ethnarchs. We can, it is true, detect two stages in Simon's power; he was at first nominated High Priest by Demetrius, but in 140 B.C. a national assembly decreed that he and his sons should be High Priests for ever. This, indeed, would be one stage worse in Essene eyes than an individual non-Aaronic High Priest nominated by the Seleucids. Between these possibilities we must choose on the basis of the other texts, but here we may observe that revolutions usually happen when the wrong party takes power *de facto*, rather than when their power becomes *de jure*. With Hyrcanus, a contrast could be made between his initial and his later religious policies; but only from a Pharisaic standpoint, not from an Essene one.

The rule of the Wicked Priest is condemned not only as impious in general, but also specifically because he confiscated the property of Jewish apostates and the booty from surrounding nations (cf. also 4*Q Testimonia*: 'his neighbours').

Other texts relate to the building activities of the persecutor. Column IX ends thus:

> The meaning of this paggage (Hab. 2.11) concerns the Priest who . . . (a lacuna of a few lines) . . . so that its (i.e. the city's) stones were built with oppression and its wooden beams with robbery.'

A little later the commentator says (X. 9–13):

> The meaning of this passage (Hab. 2.12 f.) concerns the man who drips lies, who made many go astray so as to build a city of vanity amidst murders and to form a congregation deceitful for the sake of its glory—involving many in a vain

cult and instructing them (?) in deceitful acts. But their toil will be in vain, because they will be brought to justice by fire, because they tried to cover with ignominy and shame God's chosen ones.

In the first of these passages, 'the Priest' is presumably the Wicked Priest. In the second comes a different epithet which might be translated 'pseudo-prophet'. It is reminiscent of others which occur in the *Damascus Document*. As can easily be seen, these passages use phrases similar to those we found in the quotation from the *Psalms of Joshua,* describing the construction of 'this city'. For example, in both we have civil struggles and disorders, and the reconstruction of a city 'of vanity' is linked with the origins of a group hostile to our sect. The hostile attitude of this group is expressed in general terms only—details about the persecution of the chosen ones are given in other passages.

The most discussed of these (XI. 4–8) runs thus:

> Its meaning (Hab. 2.15) concerns the Wicked Priest who persecuted the Teacher of Righteousness, trying in angry fury to devour him in the abode of his (the Teacher's) exile. At the time of the feast of atonement, on a day of rest, he appeared before them to suppress them and make them stumble on the fast day, their sabbath of rest.

Two important details are to be noticed in this passage. The Teacher of Righteousness with his followers is living somewhere outside Jerusalem. Whatever the group's reason for abandoning the Holy City, they considered their settlement as a place of exile; the identification with Qumrân seems plausible. The other extremely important feature was first explained by S. Talmon.[1] The congregation of the Teacher of Righteousness was following a different calendar from that observed in Jerusalem whence the Wicked Priest came. On no feast-day are the Jews allowed to travel more than a very short distance. But the day of atonement for the Teacher's followers did not prevent the Wicked Priest from travelling to the Essenes' 'abode of exile'. Whatever other reasons the Wicked Priest may have had, his main aim was to make the Essenes do things inconsistent with the strict observance

[1] *Biblica* XXXII, 1951, pp. 549–63.

of their calendar ('make them stumble on the fast day, their sabbath of rest').

The word *haqqiryah* ('the city') in Hab. 2.17 gives the commentator occasion to describe the evil doings of the Wicked Priest in Jerusalem (column XII. 7–9):[1]

> The meaning of 'the city' is Jerusalem, where the Wicked Priest[2] wrought abominations and defiled the sanctuary of God.

For his evil doings the persecutor receives an appropriate reward, in keeping with the well-loved doctrine *de morte persecutorum*. In commenting on Hab. 2.17 the writer observes: God will sentence him to extermination because he schemed to exterminate poor ones (*'bywnym*).[3]

A difficult passage is found in VIII. 16–IX. 2:

> The explanation of this passage relates to the Priest who rebelled and transgressed the commands (of God . . . and they) did violence to him because of his impious acts and inflicted horrible pains on him, taking their revenge upon the flesh of his body.

Unfortunately a lacuna leaves a certain margin of uncertainty. Does the 'him' after the gap refer to the subject of the beginning of the comment? Dupont-Sommer preferred to see in it an allusion to tortures inflicted on the *Teacher of Righteousness*. But since (*a*) it is more normal to suppose the same person is being discussed throughout the whole passage, and (*b*) the vocabulary is identical with that used in other passages where the death of the Wicked Priest is alluded to, we consider the passage to refer *in toto* to the persecutor.

Against F. M. Cross it must be observed that it is difficult to see in this very strong expression a swift death. The insistence on the details of the vengeance exacted on 'the flesh of his body' seems to indicate clearly that the priest was tortured and humiliated before being killed. Simon was probably too drunk to notice

---

[1] We saw that in 4*Q Testimonia* 'this city' also referred to Jerusalem.

[2] The word 'wicked' is added above the line. We have seen before that 'the Priest' alone refers to the persecutor of the sect.

[3] This word, Ebionites, is used from the later half of the second century A.D. onwards as a name for the Judaeo-Christians.

what was happening to him. As Dupont-Sommer saw, the description fits well the last years of the reign of Hyrcanus II, who was mutilated by the Parthians in 40 B.C. and strangled, by Herod the Great's orders, in 30. However, as we have observed above, he lived too late to be taken into consideration as the original persecutor of the sect. It is historically plausible that the circumstances of Jonathan's death also fit this description. That he was tortured, it is true, is not mentioned by Josephus, but it is a most probable deduction. By spreading rumours of terrible pains inflicted on the flesh of Jonathan's body, the Syrian Trypho could play for a capitulation on the part of Simon, the prisoner's brother. Seeing this plan fail, he satisfied his vengeance by putting the unfortunate captive to a painful death (pHab IX. 9–12). The whole passage deserves citing:

> Its meaning concerns the Wicked Priest whom God delivered into the hands of his enemies because he sinned against the Teacher of Righteousness and the men of his party. They afflicted him with cruel blows, so that he ended his life in bitterness of soul because he had done wrong against his (God's) chosen ones.

Here again it is difficult to see the description of an easy death. The persecutor was captured by his enemies and ill-treated for some time before he died. This treatment led to his death *bmrwry npš* 'in bitterness of soul',[1] which implies a protracted anguish. It is an end which fits Jonathan better than anyone else.

Vermès and Cross have seen an allusion to Simon's death in a drunken stupor in XI. 12–15. Cross translates it as follows:

> This means the Priest whose dishonour was greater than his honour. For he did not circumcise the foreskin of his heart but walked in ways of drunkenness (lit. well-wateredness) in order to quench his thirst (*bdrky hrwwh lm'n spwt hṣm'h*). But the cup of God's wrath will swallow him up . . .

An allusion to drunkenness can be read in the text, but if so the rest of the sentence becomes unintelligible; the Hebrew cannot

---

[1] In a fragment of a calendar giving the dates of certain historical events, *mrwry npš* can be read on one line, and below *'ṣyrym*, 'captives'. It is possible that we have here a mention of an annual commemoration of the Wicked Priest's death.

be translated 'in order to quench his thirst'. The whole phrase is derived from Deut. 29.18 (EVV: 29.19): 'to devastate the dry and the irrigated land together', and is repeated in the curse on apostates in 1Q S II. 14, in a metaphorical sense. We consider it to be so used here too, just as 'he did not circumcise the foreskin of his heart'. Accordingly, we do not find in this passage any allusion to the historical circumstances of the Wicked Priest's death but only to his unfaithfulness.

A very important passage (V. 9–12) contains an allusion to a named historical person who is explicitly set in the context of these events.

> Its meaning concerns the House of Absalom and the men of his party who remained inactive during the persecution of the Teacher of Righteousness, and did not help him against the Man of Lies, when he despised the Law, in the midst of all their congregation.

W. H. Brownlee sees in this passage a symbolic use of the name of David's son, but Freedman[1] is surely right in denying such a use, the situations being so very different. He cites two historical persons with the name of Absalom, the first being the father of a family active in the time of Simon and Jonathan, and the second a son of John Hyrcanus, who together with his nephew, Aristobulus II, was taken to Rome by Pompey in 63.[2] Freedman gives both as probable, inclining rather towards the earlier; but since all the other allusions have led us to the early Hasmonean period we can make the identification with more confidence. The 'House of Absalom' (note, not Absalom himself) played an important role in early Maccabean history. During the disaster in the plain of Ḥaṣor (I Macc. 11.69 f.),

> all the soldiers of Jonathan fled, no one remained with the exception of Mattathias, son of Absalom, and Judas, son of Halpi, who were generals of his forces.

The same family is mentioned in another passage (I Macc. 13.11) where Simon sends

[1] *BASOR* 114, April 1949, p. 11 ff.
[2] *Ant.* XIV.IV, 71; cf. *War* I. VII, 154.

Jonathan, the son of Absalom, and a considerable body of troops to Jaffa; Jonathan drove out those who were there and stayed himself.

The capture of Jaffa is considered the most striking achievement of Simon's reign (I Macc. 14.5).

Above all his (Simon's) titles to glory he took Jaffa, made it his port and opened for him access to the isles of the sea.[1]

The last passage of the *Habakkuk Commentary* (II. 1–3) pertinent for our investigation uses the same terminology that we found in the *Damascus Document*.

This passage refers to the traitors and to the Man of Lies who did not [receive] the rain [corrected to: the Teacher] of righteousness[2] sent from God; and it also refers to those who acted treacherously towards the New Covenant.

OTHER ALLUSIONS

In fragments of the commentaries on other biblical books some further allusions to the earliest moments in sectarian history have also turned up. The most important of these are found in a *pešer* on some Psalms. Its date is certainly post-Herodian. In one fragment[3] we read:

The Wicked watches for the righteous and seeks [*to slay him. But the Lord will not abandon him to his power, nor*] *condemn him when he is judged* (Ps. 37.32f.). This refers to the Wicked Priest who wat[ched for the Teacher of Righteousness and sought] to slay him . . . But God will not abandon him to his power, nor condemn him when he is judged. God will render him (i.e. the Wicked Priest) his recompense, giving

[1]Probably II Macc. 11.17 refers to this Absalom himself (although the Greek transliteration of the name is anomalous) who was acting as an envoy of Judas Maccabeus to Lysias, tutor and prime minister of Antiochus IV.

[2]We prefer this supplement and translation rather than the generally accepted one, 'who did not [believe in, or, listen to the words of] the Teacher of Righteousness'. The scribe first wrote *mwrh ṣdqh*, a direct allusion to the expression in Joel 2.23: 'For he has given you rain in due quantity' (*mwrh lṣdqh*). It should be noticed that in the title 'Teacher of Righteousness' *ṣdq* and *hṣdq* are used, but never *ṣdqh*. However, the scribe changed this last noun by adding the definitive article, so making the indefinite expression into an allusion to a person.

[3]*JBL* LXXV, 1956, p. 94.

him into the hands of cruel Gentiles to wreak (vengeance) upon him.

Here we find the theme (cf. also pHab XII. 2 above) of the persecutor receiving his just reward. An important detail is given in the phrase, 'giving him into the hands of cruel Gentiles'. The Wicked Priest is put to death by non-Jews. This detail fits perfectly the circumstances of Jonathan's death but hardly those of Simon's. Even if 'Ptolemy, son of Abubus' (Sem. Ḥabûb) were an Idumean, no one not of the Jewish religion would receive the important office that he had, and be son-in-law of the High Priest Simon. Cross, it is true, explains this feature as referring to a quite hypothetical Seleucid complicity in Simon's death, but his interpretation is scarcely natural. A second point to be noticed is the phrase, found in the biblical text and probably to be restored in the commentary, 'seeking to slay him'. The Wicked Priest tried to kill the Teacher of Righteousness, but did not succeed.

One should also notice some scattered allusions to historical or political events which, although they are more easily identifiable, seem to have little bearing on the history of the sect *sensu stricto*. Each of these events will be found in its appropriate place in the chronological table.

In a *Commentary on Nahum* we find the phrase: 'the Kings of Yawan (Greece) from Antiochus until the appearance of the rulers of the Kittiim'. This Antiochus is certainly Antiochus IV Epiphanes, who unleashed the religious persecutions in Judaea that provoked the Maccabaean revolt. In another line we find a reference to 'Demetrius, king of Yawan, who tried to enter Jerusalem on the advice of those who seek after smooth things'. Rowley has proposed that this refers to Demetrius I, but Cross makes the suggestion of Allegro, that it was Demetrius III, more plausible.[1]

'King of Yawan' and 'Kings of Yawan' in this commentary are clearly Seleucid monarchs. The title recurs in CD VIII. 9 ff.:

> about whom God said: *'Their wine is the venom of serpents and the cruel poison of asps.'* The serpents are the king of the

[1] H. H. Rowley, *JBL* LXXV, 1956, pp. 188–93 and F. M. Cross, *Library*, pp. 92–4.

nations and their wine is their ways. And the poison (*r's*) of asps is the chief (*r's*) of the kings of Yawan who has come (or: shall come) to wreak vengeance upon them.

Here too the kings of Yawan must be Seleucid kings, although the historical event referred to is obscure.

In the *Commentary on Nahum* we read:

> This passage refers to the Lion of Wrath who wreaked vengeance on the seekers after smooth things, and who used to hang men alive on trees, as was never done before in Israel, for he who is hanged alive on a tree . . .

Here we have a clear allusion to the time of Jannaeus, who, Josephus tells us, once crucified 800 Pharisees in a day. It should be noticed that by a curious twist of history the enemies of the Lion of Wrath ('those who seek after smooth things') are the same who were opposed to the Teacher in the days of the sect's foundation. An identification of them with the Pharisees and their forerunners meets these conditions.[1]

Among the manuscripts of Cave IV there is an Essene calendar giving the dates of certain historical events which were celebrated annually. This work is exceedingly fragmentary and little more can be gathered from it except that it mentions *Šalamṣiyôn* (the Hebrew name of Queen Alexandra, the successor of Alexander Jannaeus), Hyrcanus (but in such a fragmentary context that we cannot say which of the two Hyrcani is intended) and a massacre by '*mlyws* (Aemilius Scaurus, the first Roman Governor of Syria).

In the *Commentaries on Nahum, Hosea* and *Psalm* 37,[2] we have numerous allusions to 'the men of Ephraim and Manasseh', considered in most cases as enemies of the sect. In addition to the general anti-Samaritan feeling of Judaeans, there may be an allusion here to some specific conflict between them and the Essenes; but on this point our historical sources fail to inform us.[3]

---

[1]If this identification is correct, Strugnell tentatively suggests that the title *dwršy hhlqwt* is a punning allusion (*halàkôt, halāqôt*) to the Pharisees' study (√)*drš* of Halakah.

[2]*JBL* LXXV, 1956, pp. 93–95.

[3]The identification (proposed in the French edition of this book) of 'the men of Ephriam and Manasseh' with the troops of Samaritan and Trans-jordanian Jews who put down the Jewish rising of 4 B.C. seems too narrow and secular to account for the frequency of the polemic against them.

THE TEACHER OF RIGHTEOUSNESS

We are ill informed about the life and work of the Teacher of Righteousness. Neither this title nor the name of the founder of the Essenes are found in the writings of Greek and Latin historiographers, and it is hopeless for us to try to identify him with a known figure. In this connexion we should remember that Josephus hardly mentions John the Baptist and Jesus; his interest lay in other things. From two texts[1] it is clear that the Teacher was a priest, and other passages suggest that he was the sect's founder. But it is also clear that the movement's origins go back before his time, and that they were at least interested in a prehistory that preceded by about twenty years the appearance of the Teacher. We shall attempt later to identify the circumstances surrounding the historical figure and activity of the Teacher; but first we should try to depict his character. The picture that we shall get of the typical Essene outlook will also be of use for our reconstruction of the sect's beginnings, its *raison d'être*, and its development.

If it be granted that the Hymns (*Hôdāyôt*) are, at least in part, a composition of the Teacher of Righteousness, one can look in them for allusions to his life—although their phraseology is somewhat vague and heavily dependent on the texts of the Prophets and the Psalter.

From his childhood on he has been vouchsafed many special graces, God being for him both father and mother.

> For better than my father dost thou know me
> And from the womb [. . . more than] my mother hast thou cherished me.
> Since my youth thou hast revealed thyself to me in the wisdom of thy commandments.
> Thou hast given me an unshakeable faith to uphold me
> And by thy Holy Spirit thou hast made me to rejoice . . .
> For my father has not known me,

---

[1] '. . . when they heard all that was to come upon the last generation from the mouth of the priest whom God sent . . . to explain all the words of his servants the prophets' (pHab II.7–8).

'The passage refers to the priest, the Teacher of . . .' (pPs 37.23 f., published in *PEQ*, 1954, p. 72).

My mother has given me over into thy care.
Yea, thou art a father to all thy children who trust in thee,
Thou takest great pleasure in them, like her who cherishes
her nursling,
And like a foster-father thou fondlest all thy creatures in thy
bosom (1Q H IX. 29–32, 34–36).

His moral attitude corresponds to what would be expected in a
man with such a high sense of his calling, and he grows to be a
spiritual leader to his brethren:

As for me, I have known thy immense goodness
And I have sworn an oath
Not to sin against thee
Nor to commit any evil in thy sight.
Thus have I been brought into the society of the members
of my community.
Yea, according to the measure of their understanding, I
bring them in
And according to their portion in the inheritance (of God's
grace) I love them (1Q H XIV. 17–19).

God has granted him a special illumination, and infused him with
knowledge of the divine mysteries.

I thank thee, O Lord,
For thou enlightenest me with thy Covenant
[. . .] I seek after thee
And in faithfulness thou appearest unto me,
As the day-star at the first glimmerings of the day (1Q H.
IV. 5 f.).
I thank thee, O Lord,
For thou hast granted me understanding of thy faith,
And hast instructed me in thy marvellous mysteries (1Q H.
VII. 26 f.).

This divine knowledge he imparts to others, despite the persecution and trials which make him a 'sign that is spoken against'.

Through me thou hast given light to many,
And manifested thy boundless power,
For thou hast instructed me in thy unfathomable mysteries.

In thy inscrutable plan thou hast deigned to be magnified
by me,
To strike wonder into many.
All this hast thou done for thy glory,
And to make thy strength known to all the living (1Q H
IV. 27 f.).
I am a snare to the apostate, but salvation for the penitent,
Wisdom to the simple and encouragement for the feeble-
hearted
Thou hast made me a thing to be laughed at and scorned by
traitors,
But a trustworthy and keen-sighted counsellor to upright
men. . . .
Thou hast made of me a banner round whom the righteous
elect rally,
And an acknowledged interpreter of thy unfathomable
mysteries,
So as to put to the test thy children who trust thee
And to try those who love instruction.
I am a prosecutor of those who expound lying messages,
And an accuser of all short-sighted seers (1Q H II. 8–10,
13–15).[1]

Persecuted by false teachers and prophets, he, the true teacher,
is driven into exile. His conventional title, Teacher of Righteousness, which we too use for convenience, is indeed more exactly
to be translated. 'The Legitimate Teacher'.

They did not reckon that I was the instrument of thy power,
And so they chased me from my homeland like a bird from
his nest;
And all my friends were driven away from me.
They rejected me as an ill-formed vessel,
And lying interpreters, false seers,
They wove a plot against me,
To make me to exchange thy law,
Which thou hast graven in my heart,
For the things that lead thy people astray.

[1] On persecutions, cf. further V. 14, 22 ff.; VI. 8; VIII. 27 ff.

76

They hold back from the waters of knowledge those who
desire them,
And to slake their thirst they give them only vinegar (1Q H
IV. 8–11).

But finally, after the storms of persecution comes the calm.

The poor thou hast tested in the smelting pot, like gold in
the refiner's fire,
Thou hast purified him seven times, like silver that the smith
refines in the furnace.
The wicked have been eager to inflict indignities upon me,
All the day long they have ground down my soul.
But thou, my God, thou hast brought calm after the
storm,
And hast saved the soul of the poor . . . (1Q H V. 16–18).

His experience and trials have made him a father to the Pious
ones:

Thou hast appointed me to the service of thy Covenant,
And through thy promise I stand firm therein.
Thou hast made me to be a father to all the children of
Piety (*bny ḥsd*)
A foster-father to men of good omen (*'nšy mwpt*).[1]
They open their mouth as the nursling [to his mother's
breasts]
And rejoice like a child in the lap of his foster-father.
Thou hast exalted my horn against those who once despised
me,
My enemies are as the straw swept away by the wind . . .,
For thou, O my God, thou art an everlasting light to me,
Thou hast planted my feet firm on the plains of eternity
(1Q H VII. 19–23, 25).

It has been mentioned above that the Teacher of Righteousness,
the group's founder, was a Priest. The same must be said of the
members of the sect's hierarchy, who showed themselves proud
of their title of Sons of Zadok (*bny ṣdwq*), as were the Sadducees

---

[1] *bny ḥsd* may be an allusion to the name Ḥasidim. The phrase *'nšy mwpt*
derives from Zech. 3.8, where it is a title of the High Priest's companions,
to whom the Davidic Messiah will appear.

of the Gospels. The Essenes come from a priestly milieu. The political reasons for the schism which led them to quit Jerusalem are not known to us. From the sect's books, and from those of the pseudepigrapha which bear the Essene hallmark, we know that the moral conduct of the Jerusalem priests (greed and luxury) and their mode of life ('Hellenizing' tendencies) were the object of severe criticism (pHab IX. 4 ff.; Greek *Test. Levi* 14, partly attested in 4Q fragments). Indeed, it is not surprising that a breath of asceticism and a desire for a stricter religious life made itself felt among some of the priests. But for those aspirations to attain expression in a clearly defined system of faith and conduct, the intervention of a strong personality was needed; and in the Teacher of Righteousness we find him. The programme that he offered to the priesthood and laity seemed to meet the needs of the hour. He taught how men should prepare themselves to be worthy members of the new Israel, how they should play their part in God's plan of salvation, as the prophets had foretold it. Those whom God had chosen to be members of the new people were to undergo themselves the experience of their forefathers, who lived forty years in the desert before entering the Promised Land. More conscious than their fathers of man's congenital weakness, they put their trust in God's help and hoped to be enabled by it to overcome the forces of the Evil One, which at that juncture of world history were as powerful as those of Good.

According to the Teacher, a communal way of life in seclusion provided the conditions necessary to enable man to overcome his weakness in the face of the Evil One. It alone gave him a foretaste of that life among the angels in which they would share in the fullness of time. The end would surely come, once the faithful had accomplished the forty years of testing in the desert. But during this time, unlike the Children of Israel of old who by their rebellious nature and lack of order jeopardized God's plan, they would be subjected to a rigorous discipline where no fault would escape unpunished. The end of this period was to be marked by a final crisis, a war when the hosts of light and those of darkness would join battle.

Therefore the Teacher led his followers out of public life and into exile at Qumrân, where they were probably left in peace by the rulers of Jerusalem after the initial persecutions of the schism. It is worth stressing that the repeated acts of hostility shown by the Hasmoneans towards the Pharisees, whose influence among the people was growing to the detriment of the royal family's prestige, should not make us assume that these monarchs displayed the same attitude towards the Essenes. At least after the death of the Teacher the Essenes probably continued undisturbed in their way of life, inheriting from him an oral catechesis and perhaps some writings such as the *Rule of the Community* and the *Hôdâyôt*.

There has been considerable speculation about the death of the Teacher. Although in a fragmentary passage from a *pešer* on Ps. 37 it is clearly asserted that when the Wicked Priest sought to kill the Teacher 'God did not deliver him into his hands', some writers have assumed and even asserted that he was put to death by his enemies. In fact, no text clearly affirms that the Teacher suffered a violent death; the *Damascus Document,* in mentioning his death, uses the expression, 'was gathered in' (CD VIII. 21, XIX. 35, XX. 14). But this is to be understood as an abbreviation of the biblical phrase, 'he was gathered in to his fathers', used of the Patriarchs and other biblical figures who died in peace, 'full of years' (cf. Gen. 25.8; 35.29; 49.29; Deut. 32.50; Judg. 2.10). More rarely the same verb is used alone without the rest of the expression, just as we find it in the *Damascus Document*. In Num. 20.26 we read that 'Aaron will be gathered in and die there (on Mount Hor)'; in this case, too, a natural death is intended. In the Hebrew text of Ben Sira (8.7; 40.28 [29]) the word refers to death and it is not specified whether it is violent or not, while in Is. 57.1 and Hos. 4.3. it has to be made clear by the context that the death is caused by suffering.

Some scholars have sought to strengthen the case for a violent death by citing other texts. One such is the passage mentioned above from the *pešer* on Nahum, where crucifixions are mentioned. However, in the whole of this commentary, which is fairly extensively preserved, there is no allusion to events happening to the sect, much less to the Teacher of Righteousness. In another frequently cited 'proof-text', from the *Habakkuk Commentary* (cf. p. 68 above) scholars like Dupont-Sommer are compelled to postulate a change of subject, from the Wicked Priest to the Teacher, in order to make the prophecies of doom refer to the

Teacher in this passage, although verbatim recollections of this passage in other places (e.g. pHab IX. 9–12) refer incontestably to the Wicked Priest.

To sum up, in no place do the texts speak of, nor presuppose, a violent death of the Teacher of Righteousness; they rather favour the hypothesis that he died naturally. Moreover, whatever the historical truth may have been, the fact and manner of the Teacher's death had for the Essenes no theological nor soteriological significance analogous to that seen by the early Church in the death of Jesus of Nazareth.

SYNTHESIS

With this evidence before us, it is time to attempt a coherent picture of the origins and development of the Essenes. We must try to combine the Essenes' writings, the archaeological evidence and the references to them found in classical writers. The interpretation of many details may be inexact, but for the decisive moments of this history, where the evidence is more abundant, we expect to be on moderately firm ground. We insist on the growth that is to be observed in tenets and organization, a growth which is rapid in the first generations but which slows down towards the end. For some details of the evidence for doctrinal development, the reader must refer to the following chapter.

'THEY WERE LIKE THE BLIND . . . FOR TWENTY YEARS'

It is clear from the *Damascus Document* that the appearance of the Teacher was preceded by a period of some twenty years, which the sect regarded as in some sense part of their history. When one tries to give a name to these 'Proto-Essenes', one thinks immediately of the Asidaeans (Ḥasidim) of the Maccabean period.[1] This pietist movement combined a fierce nationalism with

---

[1] That the word Ḥasidim is also used as a name for the Essenes seems to follow from a text which will shortly be published. The synonymous use of 'Ḥasidim' and 'Essenes' supports the derivation of this latter word from the Aramaic *ḥăsên, ḥăsayyâ* the plurals of *ḥasyâ*, 'pious'. This etymology could not formerly be maintained without qualification because of the *prima facie* strong objection that the Aramaic word was only found in Syriac and never attested in any West Aramaic dialect. But it has been generally overlooked that the verb was found by Cantineau in a Palmyrene inscription meaning, in the pa'el, 'he consecrated' (*Syria* XIV, 1933, p. 177). In this case, the use of its participle in Jewish Aramaic is not improbable.

a religious, namely messianic, fervour. A group drawn from priesthood and laity, its origins may go back as far as the early post-exilic period, but it began to show its full vitality after the time of Antiochus Epiphanes' persecution (I Macc. 2.42; 7.13–17). In the crucial year 167, this resistance group joined forces with that of the Maccabees; one group mainly religious, opposed to the cultic and cultural consequences of the impact of the Hellenistic world, and the other group centred round the Maccabean family, which was from the start military and soon became political in its aims. It is significant that during the course of the war the Asidaeans broke with the Maccabees, abandoned resistance to the Seleucid King and supported Alcimus, his ungodly but Aaronite nominee to the high priesthood:

> The Asidaeans were the first from the children of Israel to seek peace with them, for they said: a priest from the race of Aaron has come with the troops and he will do us no harm (I Macc. 7.13 f.).

From their religious standpoint the restoration of a legitimate descendant of the Aaronite line of priests was a sufficient victory in the war. Their 'blindness and groping' were only increased when Alcimus and his Greek patrons turned upon them and slaughtered sixty of them (cf. also II Macc. 14.6 ff.). Rather than identify Asidaeans and Essenes, it seems more plausible to assume that within the vast Asidaean movement a certain group of more precise tendencies crystalized and, at a point of time which we will try to determine more exactly, the Essene group may be said to have emerged.

The author of I Maccabees, being a court historian or at least a supporter of the reigning family, was only interested in the doings of Mattathias and his sons. It can, however, be safely

---

For a refutation of two other etymologies cf. F. M. Cross, *Library*, p. 37, n. 1. In connexion with the reign of Alexander Jannaeus, a Samaritan chronicle of the Middle Ages mentions the three Jewish sects of Pharisees, Sadducees and Ḥasidim. These last, it is true, are identified by the Chronicler with the Samaritans (E. Vilmar, *Abulfathi Annales Samaritani*, Gotha 1865, p. 102; 11.11–13 in the Arabic text). The use of these names could derive from the account of the Jewish sects in John Hyrcanus' reign, either in the Hebrew Josippon, or in the Arabic version of it (where they occur as *'lfrwsym, 'lsdwqyt, 'lhsdym*). Cf. on the Arabic Version, G. Graf, *Gesch. der Christlichen Arabischen Literatur* I, 1944 (*Studi e Testi* 118), pp. 221–3.

deduced that Mattathias and his supporters represented quite a small group in the beginning, insignificant in comparison with the already established congregation of the Asidaeans. Even though they are hardly mentioned, we may guess that other families as well as the Maccabees (like the House of Absalom mentioned above) played an important part in the war of liberation. But the growing prestige of the Hasmonean family led inevitably to a conflict with the Asidaeans. I Maccabees gives us glimpses of this struggle and we find allusions to it at the end of the twenty year period at the beginning of the *Damascus Document*. In pHab V, 9–12) we find references to the critical phase of this conflict, when the non-Aaronite Hasmonaeans took over the priesthood. The Asidaeans were not by definition a military body, and in their struggle against the Hasmonaeans they had to look for a family which had some military strength. The House of Absalom, of high military and political distinction, had probably shown sympathy with their religious aims, but for some unknown reason decided to support the Hasmonaean family at this juncture. Accordingly, the Asidaeans are eliminated at this period as serious candidates for political power, and part of them, whom we may now call the Essenes, abandoned Jerusalem for an exile at Qumrân. The consequent change in the political situation of Jerusalem results in the appearance of the division into three parties which lasted until after the turn of the era, and which probably dates from this period; at least it is about the time of Jonathan that Josephus first mentions this division. When the Essenes abandoned politics, there were left the pro-Hasmonaeans the Sadducees and those members of the religious group who had not considered the question of the priesthood of the Maccabees to be a matter *stantis aut cadentis ecclesiae,* but who progressively grew colder to the ruling family because of more empirical questions of politics and *halakah.*[1]

Several possible motives could have led to the withdrawal and exodus of the Essenes. Their disapproval of the impact of Hellenism has already been mentioned, but with a sect of priestly origin

[1]Interesting remarks on the Asidaeans and the Great Assembly (*Keneset Haggedôlâh*), known from rabbinic texts, can be found in L. Finkelstein, *Happerûšîm we'anšê Keneset Haggedôlâh* (Transactions of the Jewish Theological Society of America XV), New York 5710/1950, although his treatment of our period is rather perfunctory.

we look naturally for more religious and strictly cultic grounds of schism, e.g., disapproval of the illegitimate origin of the ruling priests and of their unworthy conduct. In the Essenes' texts we find a vehement insistence on the authority of their cultic calendar; in default of another cause of schism we could infer, unfortunately without any clear evidence in other sources, that one of the early Hasmonaeans opposed the Teacher by making, or failing to make, some drastic reforms in the official cultic calendar. The question of the non-Aaronite descent of the Hasmonaeans would, of course, be a sufficient reason for schism; but it is never clearly mentioned in the texts, although the reference to the Asidaeans in I Maccabees makes it plausible that they dissented on this ground too. Their writings are full of complaints about wicked and unworthy conduct. In a normal moral sense this would be insufficient reason for a priestly schism; but there may have been some specific cultic transgression which escapes us in the stereotyped phraseology.[1] As a result of a situation where all these grievances were felt, either voluntarily or under compulsion, the Essenes abandoned the Holy City, which became for them a City of Vanity.

FIRST PHASE: STRICT ESSENISM

The excavators distinguish two phases in the first period of Essene occupation at Qumran, Ia and Ib. During Phase Ia one round cistern, dating from the eighth century B.C., was re-used, and near it two rectangular cisterns were dug, all three drawing their water from the rain that fell on the plateau. Modest structures were erected around these centres of water supply; and a surrounding 'casemate' type of wall, also of the Iron II period, was re-used.

It was therefore only a small group of voluntary exiles, consisting of intransigent priests and laymen from the 'Pious Ones', that first settled in the desert. The traces of the earliest occupation are exceedingly sparse and were only detected by very close analysis of the remains of the walls. The later building activity would in any case have obliterated most of the structures existing

---

[1] The expression 'defiling the sanctuary' seems to refer, in CD V. 6–8, to sexual intercourse with menstruants and the marriage of a man with his niece.

before. Nor is it surprising that only a few coins dating from this period have been found. Since they were a small group, their isolation from the world and dependence on their own products could be much more thorough-going than was possible for the larger later community. Furthermore, in many excavations, parallels can be found for this relatively scarce attestation of the first years of occupation. One can cite the excavations of a near-by and similarly monastic settlement. In the ruins of the Byzantine monastery of St Euthymius, near the modern road from Jerusalem to Jericho, Chitty's excavations did not detect any traces of the earliest phase of its existence, during the life of the founder himself. But as we know from literary sources (i.e. Cyril of Scythopolis), there was a modest central building surrounded by hermits' dwellings. All that could be found were the imposing remains of structures built after the founder's death, when the *laura* was replaced by a *coenobium* and relations with the outside world became closer.[1]

We may confidently set the beginning of period I*b* in the reign of Hyrcanus I; but archaeology gives us only a *terminus ante quem* for the initial occupation and offers no objective criterion for the length of this first phase. To establish this, we must use literary evidence and try to date the 'founding events' of the sect, the conflict of the Teacher of Righteousness with the priests of Jerusalem. In trying to identify the chief opponent of the sect, the Wicked Priest, we detected two important facts: that the Wicked Priest rebuilt Jerusalem, and that he died in torment after captivity. Whereas many other traits fitted several of the Hasmonaean priest-rulers, these two fit only Jonathan (160–42), fifth of the sons of Mattathias, successor of Judas Maccabaeus. He managed in a few years to surmount the crisis caused by the Jewish disaster at Bir-zeit in which Judas had met his death. After Demetrius I Soter had made important concessions to Jonathan, he fortified Mount Zion with a wall of hewn stones surrounding the whole temple esplanade, and began to reconstruct the sectors of the town devastated under Jason and Menelaus. Demetrius' rival, Alexander Balas, won Jonathan over to his side by bestowing on him the high priesthood in 152 B.C., and shortly afterwards

[1] D. J. Chitty, *PEQ*, 1928, pp. 134–52, 175–8; 1930, pp. 188–203; and A. Barrois, *RB* XXXIX, 1930, pp. 272–5.

he made him Strategos and Meridarch of Judaea (150/49). Accordingly, it is towards 152 that we must date the critical change in Jonathan's career. Before that time he had been a faithful executor of the policy of independence and isolation initiated by his father and brothers, a policy which seemed to contribute to the realization of an ideal dear to the hearts of faithful Jews and especially the Ḥasidim, namely that of restoring the Kingdom of God. After that date, however, he became involved in the complicated game of Syrian politics, and was primarily interested in carving out for himself a slice of the disintegrating Seleucid empire. Demetrius I's concessions, which resulted in the rebuilding of Jerusalem, in restoring to the Greek King the right of appointing the High Priest, in Jonathan's nomination as military and civil chief of Judaea, and Antiochus VI's later appointment of him as governor of Syria—these are the stages in his 'abandoning God and betraying his commandments'.

Jonathan had no difficulty in finding people to support him in this process of secularization which completely perverted the ideal of the Holy War. But against him and his 'congregation', devoted to 'the service of vanity' and 'works of folly' (pHab X. 11 f.), rose up the Ḥasidim and especially a number of priests, scandalized to see a non-Aaronite, and a robber chieftain to boot, appointed as their High Priest. One of them, the Teacher of Righteousness, preached a break with these traitors to their faith and nation, announcing that God's plan could not come to fulfilment unless they separated themselves totally from the apostates and wicked ones among the people. This was the time that the exodus to Qumrân took place. A visit of Jonathan to Qumrân proved an especially memorable point in the prince's attempts to reduce these centres of passive resistance; but his efforts failed. God saved his chosen ones and their Master, while their persecutor was severely punished. In 143 Trypho, the general of Alexander Balas and the guardian of his son Antiochus VI, captured Jonathan at Ptolemais by treachery. In the following year, after the failure of his campaign against Simon, he withdrew to Antioch and had Jonathan executed.

The identification of the Wicked Priest with Jonathan was first proposed by G. Vermès.[1] But he considered that the

[1] *Cahiers Sioniens* VII, 1953, pp. 71–74; *Discovery in the Judaean Desert*, pp. 90–97.

expression 'Wicked Priest' denoted also Simon, Jonathan's successor. He associates the visit of the Wicked Priest to Qumrân with the period of office of the latter (pHab XI. 4–8), as well as his building activities (X. 9–13) and his death in drunkenness (XI. 12).

Cross[1] has developed this viewpoint, identifying the persecutor uniquely with Simon. The following principal criticisms of this thesis should be made. First of all, in the *Psalms of Joshua,* the building activity of two brothers is mentioned. Cross has to assume that these are the two sons of Simon; but for their building activity there is no support in either Josephus or Maccabees. Such activity, however, is attested for the two brothers, Jonathan and Simon; in this case we have to place at least the beginning of enmity in the reign of the first of the two. Secondly, the impressive allusions to the manner of the persecutor's death have to be taken in a watered-down sense in the hypothesis of Simon. The quick murder of the drunken Simon by Jewish officials hardly accounts for such expressions as 'God delivered him into the hands of his enemies', 'the cruel ones of the pagans', who 'wrought horrible ills upon the flesh of his body', so that he 'died in bitterness of soul'. The proposed allusion to his drunken death, as we have seen, cannot in any case be translated in that way and is a simple metaphor for ungodly action which will be punished by God. Thirdly, the fact that both of the builders in the passage from the *Psalms of Joshua* are called 'vessels of violence' points certainly to a sectarian enmity towards Simon also. Cross's suggestion that his transformation of the Maccabaean high priesthood into a hereditary office was strongly opposed by the Essenes, and his interesting commentary on the honorific decree of I Macc. 14.27 ff., seem to us to give a plausible reason for a specific opposition to Simon. But if the texts force us to set the beginning of the schism in the days of Jonathan, this further abomination would merely have resulted in a new wave of exiles to Qumrân. Fourthly, we agree with Cross that the schism must have been motivated by questions of priestly ideology. But while the texts suggest that the Aaronite descent of the High Priest was important, they do not clearly state whether either the *de jure* recognition of the Hasmonaean

[1]*Library*, ch. III.

family's high priesthood under Simon, or the *de facto* possession of it under Jonathan was *the* question of dissent. Historical analogy suggests that, of the two suggestions, the latter is more probable; revolts usually occur at the stage of *de facto* innovation rather than at that of *de jure* recognition.

In favour of this identification of the Wicked Priest with Jonathan we can also use Josephus' evidence. The first passage where he mentions the Essenes is found in his treatment of Jonathan's reign. 'About that time there were among us three sects which differed among each other in their doctrine concerning men's acts: the first was the Pharisees, the second the Sadducees, and the third the Essenes' (*Ant.* XIII. v, 171).

By oral teaching and by his writings (the *Rule of the Community* and the nucleus at least of the collection of *Hymns*) the Teacher of Righteousness gave its special character to Qumrân monastic life in the first phase of strict Essenism. Indeed, the dominant ideas of the *Rule* (the mystique of the desert, the acute consciousness of man's need of God's grace, man's life in community with the angels, the foretaste of the life which is to come in the end of days) all were piously meditated upon and put into practice up to the very end of the Essene movement. But the community's organization and discipline was soon to undergo a considerable transformation.

Its messianic beliefs also had of necessity to evolve. In this initial phase they were predominantly *priestly* in character. The dominant eschatological role was attributed to the Priestly Messiah who was to found the New Jerusalem and the Heavenly Temple. For these enthusiasts for theocracy the role ascribed to the Son of David was doubtless a secondary one, if he had any part to play at all.

SECOND PHASE: ESSENISM WITH PHARISAIC NUANCES

The first generation found the modest group of buildings at Qumrân quite sufficient for their needs; the next group enlarged the monastery considerably. We are here in the archaeologists' phase Ib, the most flourishing of the occupational periods of Qumrân.

An increase in candidates called for considerable building

operations. First of all, a complex water-supply system had to be constructed, with a dam, an aqueduct and seven large cisterns. Agriculture was engaged in on a larger scale, in the oasis of 'Ain Fešḫa and perhaps elsewhere. There are no signs that this was a slow expansion; rather it seems to have been a sudden growth in the size of the community which provoked this activity. For instance, there is no intermediary stage between Phase Ia with its one large cistern and two subsidiary ones, depending on a scarce and capricious rainfall from which only some dozens of hermits could live, and the water system of Ib conceived and constructed as a unity depending on the more regular rainfall from the Buqeiʿa, and with a storage capacity sufficient for a couple of hundred persons.

This afflux of new members was caused in all probability by the religious persecution of John Hyrcanus I (134–104) which broke out towards the end of his life and which were directed against the Pharisees. It is probably he whom the (contemporary) *Damascus Document* has in mind. It gives him the scriptural title, 'He who oozes falsehood' (CD I. 14 f.; IV. 19; VIII. 13),[1] i.e., the false prophet, giving the lie to the belief in his exceptional gift of prophecy which, Josephus stresses, was widely accepted among the populace. Some features of the sect's persecutor could apply to Jonathan, but fit Hyrcanus more aptly. Thus, for instance, Jonathan may have become wealthy as a result of his successful campaigns against the sons of Yambri in the region of Madaba, the Zabadaeans in the Lebanon, Apollonius, the general of Demetrius II, Antioch, etc. And again his massacre of Seleucid collaborators among the Jews would have enabled him to fill his treasury with confiscated property (cf. I Macc. 9.61, 73). But among the Hasmonaean kings it is John Hyrcanus who, in the eyes of Josephus, is the first Hasmonaean ruler systematically to enrich the treasury. It is rather in him that we should see the 'Ruler of Israel . . . who piles up wealth', not only from his conquests ('the wealth of nations', pHab VIII. 12) but also by

---

[1] This persecutor of the sect is also called 'the Man of Falsehood' (*'iš hakkazab*; pHab II. 11; V. 11 and CD XX. 15) and 'the Man of Scorn' (*'iš hallaṣôn*: CD I. 14; XX. 11). We distinguish him from the initial persecutor of the sect who is regularly called the 'Wicked Priest', 'the Priest', 'the Priest who rebelled'.

confiscating the estates awarded by the Seleucid kings to their adherents in Palestine ('the wealth of violent men who rebelled against God', pHab VIII. 11), minting a bronze currency, and peacefully developing Judaea. Along with the confiscation went a bloody repression, the 'massacre of the renegades' commemorated by the Pharisees (cf. the calendar of *Ta'anit* for the 22nd Elul).

Commentators on the Scriptures, writing over a century later, mixed up the characteristics of the two persecutors and produced a composite picture of the typical Hasmonaean ruler, arch-enemy of the sect. So the *Commentary on Habakkuk* makes the False Prophet into the builder (X. 9–13) and the Wicked Priest into the hoarder of the wealth of the nations. One should note, however, the difference between the persecution of Jonathan and that of John Hyrcanus. The first was directed specifically against those who lived at Qumrân, and culminated in the visit of the Wicked Priest to the Teacher of Righteousness's 'abode of exile': but the second persecution only indirectly touched them in their seclusion, by considerably increasing their numbers, because they had abandoned the main struggles of Jewish politics.

When Hyrcanus turned his attention from the 'men of violence' and started persecuting the Pharisees, towards the end of his reign, as Josephus tells us, those who were ready to embrace the monastic form of life and some other Essene sympathizers took flight from the troubles of Judaea and converged upon the region of Qumrân. The death of the Teacher of Righteousness, which occurred about this time, marked the start of a new period of forty years, a clear allusion to the desert wanderings of the Hebrews. In this they saw a type of the opposition between the sinful generation of the congregation of traitors and the generation of those who repent and keep the Covenant (CD XX. 14 ff, I. 13 ff.); this opposition of two contemporary groups, rather than the dying out of an evil generation and its replacement by a good one, is derived from a prophetic viewpoint rather than from the traditions of the Pentateuch. The growth of the community and the Pharisaic background of the newcomers brought about inevitably certain institutional changes in the monastic life. Those who adhered to the older discipline of poverty withdrew somewhat to live a solitary life in huts and caves; no coin has yet been found in more than thirty caves that have shown traces of occupation in this period. Those living in the monastery or close around it were permitted to keep small coins, which accounts for the fairly large number of bronze coins found during the seasons of excavation. On entering the community they had to renounce all their property; but, as in Byzantine monasteries, this does not exclude the acquisition of small sums of money in some way or another. For infringements of the Rule, a penal code prescribed among other things that the guilty should be put on quarter-rations, a penalty doubtless already decreed by the Teacher himself.

A fairly important group left the community at Qumrân and settled in the region of Damascus, without, however, abandoning the priestly character of the movement's theology, and remaining in communion with the 'mother house'. The *Damascus Document* was drawn up to provide an appropriate rule for the life of this offshoot in the Hauran.

A similar rule was also followed by those members of Essene groups who lived in the towns and villages of Palestine. In some manuscripts of Cave IV there are collections of halakic prescriptions with no specific allusion to a community of either the Damascus or Qumrân types. It is possible that these manuscripts contain the rules for groups of 'tertiaries', copied by the expert scribes of Qumrân. Although Philo and Josephus describe certain details of the central Essene community, their idealized account of the Essene way of life is derived mainly from the practice of these scattered groups. Several passages of Josephus mention by name individual Essenes who put in an appearance at various moments in history. For instance, Judas the Essene predicts the death of Antigonus, the brother of Aristobulus I, in 104 B.C.[1] Menahem predicts for the young Herod a royal dignity; Simon explains for Archelaus, the Ethnarch, a dream which had troubled him before he was exiled. John the Essene, at the time of the first Jewish Revolt, is Toparch of Thamna and leads a

---

[1]This specific reference gives us a historical *terminus ante quem* for the foundation of the sect and automatically excludes later candidates for the title of Wicked Priest, such as Alexander Jannaeus. W. H. Brownlee even identifies this Judas with the Teacher of Righteousness; *gratis dictum, gratis negatum*.

punitive expedition against the Greek cities on the coast of Palestine.[1]

Prescriptions concerning family life, the sabbath rest and ritual purity are all characteristics which reveal the somewhat Pharisaic tendency of the new group at Damascus. The Temple is recognized and it is accepted with resignation that contact with foreigners is unavoidable. The group of camps in the region of Damascus is administered by two supervisors, one a layman and the other of Aaronite descent, while at Qumrân there is only one leader, of priestly origin. In the settlements of the Hauran, as well as at the monastery in Judaea and among the 'tertiaries' in Palestine, the laity, in varying degrees, had a part in legislative and judiciary activities as well as the priests. Although this democratic trait was to some degree already present in the Hasidic movement, it is much more typical of Pharisaism.[2]

During this period the fervour of the community seems to have subsided, and its convictions became fairly fluid. This leads us to suppose a lessening of eschatological tension, superseded by a greater emphasis on the daily observance of the law, as it was carefully determined by the sect's halakic specialists. In the apocalyptic community at Qumrân they continued to wait for the Messiah of Aaron and the Messiah of Israel, the High Priest and with him (perhaps in concession to Pharisaic and popular sentiments) the Royal Anointed. They were to preside over the

---

[1] Judas: *War* I. iii, 78–80; *Ant.* XIII. xi, 311–13; Menahem: *Ant.* XV. x, 373–79. Simon: *War* II. vii, 111–13. *Ant.* XVII. xiii, 346–8 (on the Essenes' gift for divination, cf. *War* II. viii, 159). John: *War* II. xx, 567, III. ii, 11.

[2] Even a perfunctory comparison of the *Rule* with the *Damascus Document* shows that two different ways of life are being described, although both have the same religious ideals. Some of these differences we have mentioned. It is methodologically unsound to take the phrase 'land of Damascus' and, on the strength of a quotation in CD. VII, 14 ff. of Amos 5.26 f., to see in it a symbolic name for Qumrân. We therefore take it literally. Another suggestion which tried to take 'Damascus' literally was made by de Vaux, who proposed to fill the archaeological hiatus of 31–4 B.C. by an exile in Damascus. This must be excluded on palaeographical grounds, the earliest manuscript of the *Damascus Document* certainly antedating 30 B.C. On the important Jewish Diaspora in the Hauran see B.S. Luria, *The Jews in Syria in Postexilic, Greco-Roman, and Byzantine Times* (in Hebrew), Jerusalem 1957. The region was fairly densely settled by the Jews in the Greco-Roman period, and until the fourth century many Jewish and Christian sects were to be found there.

'Eschatological' banquet that was prepared for the congregation, a banquet at which the women and children of the other communities would also be present. But attention was mainly devoted to the cultic side of the restored kingdom, which had already been sketched by the prophet Ezekiel. The *Description of the New Jerusalem* was avidly read. The same belief in two Messiahs occurs also in the *Damascus Document*, but the duality there is rather functional, for we also find traces of a belief in one messianic figure who fulfils both priestly and royal functions (XIV. 9).

Beside the Syro-Palestinian branches of the Essene movement mention should be made of the Therapeutae, known to us from Philo.[1] Their way of life was analogous to that of the Essenes, being Jewish solitaries who lived in the region of Lake Mareotis near Alexandria. In Qumrân Cave IV some fragments of the LXX have been found; this Greek translation of the Old Testament is a work of Alexandrian origin. Perhaps these fragments are a sign that a relation existed between the two groups. Another parallel between the two groups deserves notice. According to Philo, the Therapeutae had a religious feast of an unspecified type every fifty days. In reconstructing the calendar from Cave IV, I have noticed that there was also a division of the year into seven fifty-day periods, each beginning with a feast of an agricultural character; four of these feasts' names are preserved.

So from its modest beginnings in the second century B.C. the Essene movement spread widely throughout the Jewish world. At least four different branches are known to us, the celibates of Qumrân (solitaries and cenobites), the married Essenes living in isolated Jewish villages of southern Syria, the Palestinian 'Tertiaries' and the Therapeutae, Egyptian Jewish hermits.[2]

Political persecutions under Alexander Jannaeus, the 'furious lion' of the Nahum *pešer*, civil strife in Palestine and Roman interventions during the days of the last Hasmonaeans were enough to supply Qumrân and the settlements of the Hauran with a steady stream of recruits. But the apocalyptic group in the Judaean Desert gradually grew weary of waiting so long (cf.

---

[1] *De Vita Contemplativa* 21–90 and Eusebius, *Hist. Eccl.* II. 17.

[2] On the analogies between the Ḥabûrôt (companies) of orthodox Jews in antiquity, and the communities of Essenes, cf. S. Liebermann, *JBL* LXXI, 1952, pp. 199–206; C. Rabin, *Qumrân Studies*, Oxford 1957.

pHab VII. 7–8, 10–14); thus the ground was prepared for the Essenes' venture into politics in the time of Herod the Great.

THIRD PHASE: THE ESSENES DURING HEROD'S REIGN

This period is far less clear than the others. Its beginning is marked by an earthquake and a great fire which ravaged the settlement at Qumrân. The excavators consider these disasters to have been contemporaneous but there is no evidence to rule out the assumption that a short space of time lay between them. They were, according to de Vaux, followed by an abandonment of the settlement, which lasted most of the reign of Herod the Great (37–4 B.C.). It must be confessed that the evidence for this archaeological gap is somewhat tenuous. The numismatic argument is not decisive since, although only five coins of Herod's reign have been found, there are also only four from the reign of Hyrcanus II when the site was certainly occupied. More importance, however, should be attached to the above-mentioned deposit of mud about 75 cm. thick; beneath it there is a layer of ashes and, at the time when the settlement was rebuilt, the reinforcements of the north-west corner of the western building were laid on top of this layer of mud.

The earthquake, moreover, does not form a sufficient reason for the abandonment of the site. We prefer, accordingly, an explanation which takes into account also the data that contemporary history gives. The anecdote told by Josephus about Menahem the Essene, who predicted a royal destiny for the young Herod, suggests that from the start the Essenes looked favourably on the rising star of the Antipatrids and the consequent dwindling of Hasmonaean power. The affection was mutual, for the son of Antipater, foreseeing the increasing opposition of the wealthy, the Sadducees and the Pharisees, in the whole nation could rely only on the somewhat passive support of the peasantry, who enjoyed the fruits of the greater economic prosperity of his reign, and on that of the Essences, who were hostile to the ruling dynasty, the official priesthood, and the lay teachers of the Torah who followed a different Halakah. In contrast with Herod's rapidly changing attitude towards these groups, he showed a lasting friendship to the Essenes. He kept Menahem in his entourage and respected the sect's religious scruples. Josephus says, 'He always treated all the Essenes with honour' (*Ant.* XV. x, 378).

Now towards 40 B.C. Herod was going through a critical phase in his career. At that time the Parthians were in occupation of Syria and Palestine, and the Hasmonean Antigonus won them over to his side. There followed a violent repression of Herod's supporters. Herod himself took flight, first to Masada and soon afterwards to Petra, Alexandria and Rome. Among the centres of Herodian supporters destroyed by the Parthians and Antigonus between 40 and 37 we should perhaps include the monastery of Qumrân.[1] The few coins of Mattathias suggest that the destruction came rather late in this period of repression. The sectarians must have abandoned the site in haste, and the Parthian cavalry had to satisfy itself by burning down the settlement. Before leaving, the sectarians hid away their manuscripts in caves. Such a precautionary measure must have taken place once in the first century B.C.; how else can the discovery, in caves closed finally in A.D. 68 (e.g. Cave I), of Hellenistic-type lamps be explained? In the remains of the settlement such lamps are found only in the levels of the first period of occupation. It is however possible that a small Essene group continued there, scraping out a precarious existence in the ruins of the monastery; their presence would account for some of the coins of Herod found in the ruins.

During Herod's long reign the Essenes hardly took any part in the political struggles of the nation, remaining true to their attitude of abstention from worldly issues. Herod, moreover, exasperated by the immutable hostility of the Jews and relying more and more on the support of the pagan element of Palestine, must have gradually forfeited the approval of his former allies. This state of affairs, aggravated by the Jews' growing hatred of the Romans, set the scene for a new exodus to Qumrân.

FOURTH PHASE: ESSENISM WITH ZEALOT TENDENCIES

The death of Herod in 4 B.C. plunged Palestine into a terrifying chaos. The struggle against his dynasty grew into a war against the Romans. Varus, the governor of Syria, with the aid of Herod's mercenaries and some Nabataean troops, launched a rapid campaign and pacified the country.

[1]See E. M. Laperrousaz, *VT* VII, 1957, pp. 345 f.

The former inhabitants of Qumrân, accompanied by new recruits, remembered 'the days of their youth in the desert' (cf. Hos. 2.16 f., EVV 2.14 f.) and returned to their old monastery. Some of its dilapidated buildings were restored, but part of the settlement was not reoccupied, from which we see that the numbers of the group were smaller than during the former period. Some new defensive works suggest the troubled nature of the times, and perhaps a more military preoccupation with them.

The exiles, especially the younger recruits, were as much filled with anti-Roman sentiments as with religious fervour. Preparations for the war against the Kittiim assumed an important place in the life of their monastic retreat. At this time the *Rule of the War* was written, describing the period of forty years foreseen to be necessary for the total extermination of the Sons of Darkness. The drawing up of the catalogue of buried treasures was doubtless connected with these often theoretic preparations. The writer of this catalogue was not a scholar like the scribes trained in the monastery's school. He did not know literary Hebrew, and drew up his work in Mishnaic, which was at that time the spoken dialect of the inhabitants of Judaea. His hand is clumsy, his spelling swarms with mistakes.[1] Probably a Zealot, and a naïve believer in popular legends, he drew up this list of treasures which he perhaps imagined would finance the Essenes' military budget in the Holy War. The work breathes the same unrealistic atmosphere of exaltation that also characterizes the *Rule of the War*, in which a somewhat odd strategy and tactics are laid down which are to result in the extermination of all non-Jews. In both texts, they copied the numbers of non-existent armies and stores so often that they ended by believing in them. There is a noteworthy difference between the three hoards of silver tetradrachms (14 grams each) containing respectively 223, 183 and 150 coins which the excavators found, and the treasures described in the copper rolls, where amounts of silver and gold are calculated in hundreds of talents (the talent being about $34\frac{1}{4}$ kilograms or 72 pounds).

Despite this Zealot tendency life at Qumrân followed in broad outline its old pattern, although many changes in detail took place. The inhabitants of the monastery and the hermits continued to be great readers. The manuscripts that had been hidden away in

[1] See *BA* XIX, 1956, p. 62.

38 B.C. were brought out once again, and many new copies were made; among the old books, especially popular were Jubilees, Enoch, the *Rule of the Community,* the *Damascus Document* and the *Hymns*: a new phenomenon seems to be the *writing* of commentaries on the prophetic and legal parts of the Old Testament.

From the point of view of its institutions, the Essene group of the time of the procurators seems to be of a notably hybrid character. Together with the celibate members (who were mainly hermits) married people were also admitted. It is significant that the tombs of women lie on the edge of the chief cemetery, and in two smaller separate cemeteries (*RB* LXIII, 1956, pp. 569–72) showing that they date from the later period of Essene settlement at Qumrân.

A manuscript from Cave IV in the neat hand of the Herodian period may well reflect this hybrid type of life. One of its fragments contains prescriptions concerning Sabbath observance; these are identical with those of the *Damascus Document* (X. 14 ff.), but follow a different order. Another fragment gives us the end of this section of the *Damascus Document* with a passage immediately following it that corresponds, with some abbreviation, to a section of the *Rule of the Community* (VIII. 1–10, the Council of fifteen men). After this comes a paragraph giving the laws concerning purification after childbirth, derived from Lev. 12.2 f. and Jub. 3.8–14. Two other fragments contain a penal code similar to that of 1Q S VI. 24 ff. and CD XIV. 18 ff., but offenders are in this case only put on half rations, and not on quarter rations as in the stricter earlier phases. Then a few small scraps of leather give a quotation of Isa. 54.1 f., probably continuing into v. 3, where the prophet says, 'Thy seed shall possess the nations, and thy sons shall people the desolated cities.'

In their belief in the two Messiahs, the 'Offshoot of David' gains in importance over the 'Expounder of the Law', the Priestly Anointed One.[1] It is he who is the 'Prince of the Congregation' of the *War* scroll and who will march from the desert on Jerusalem, at the head of the Children of Light who live in Judaea and the diaspora (1Q M I. 2 f.). There the last battle will take place, and the Messianic Kingdom be established.

The Zealot character of the Essene community in its last

[1] *JBL* LXXV, 1956, pp. 174–81; three documents written in the first half of the first century A.D.

hase also explains why Qumrân was destroyed by the Legio X
Fretensis in the summer of 68. It had become a centre of military
resistance, or at least a school of propagandists. At that time the
majority of the sectarians fled, having once again hidden their
manuscripts as they had done in 38 B.C. Those who stayed were
massacred or captured by the Romans.

The main cemetery and the two smaller cemeteries contain in
all about 1,200 burials of adults. The age of the skeletons is
between thirty and fifty years. Within the termini that we have
accepted for the occupation at Qumrân (150 B.C.–A.D. 68), with
a hiatus of about thirty years during the reign of Herod, we have
to deal with an occupation lasting some 190 years. Assuming that
a generation lasts twenty-five to thirty years, we have between
six and eight generations that died at Qumrân during this period;
the average size of the population during any generation was then
between 150 and 200—although the settlement seems to have
been much smaller during the first generation and slightly more
flourishing in period Ib than in period II. This is, indeed, a high
number of persons to adopt so rigorous a form of life, but there
are parallels. The famous monastery of Mar Saba, in a similar
geographical setting and again under a hostile régime (that of the
Moslems), numbered 150 monks at the beginning of the ninth
century, as the *Commemoratorium de casis Dei* informs us. Philo and
Josephus both give the figure of 3,000 as the total of the Essenes
living in Palestine. Probably this represents the situation at the
beginning of our era. Accordingly at least 5 per cent lived the
strict monastic life, a rather high proportion.

The Roman attack, then, brought a brutal stop to the Essene
community's life, at least at Qumrân. After 70 they may have
vegetated for some time, but in any case the tragic result of the
Second Revolt, whose ideology in some respects was the same as
theirs, put an end to any hope of the reorganization of sectarian
life at Qumrân. The majority of the Essenes was either re-
absorbed by official Judaism, or else passed over to orthodox
Christianity or, more likely, to one of the many Gnostic sects
that flourished at that time.[1]

[1] The lists of sects preserved for us in the writings of the Fathers do not
allow us to assume that the Essenes continued to exist as an organized
group as late as the fourth century: cf. Eusebius, *Hist. Eccl.*, ed. G. Bardy,
Vol. I, p. 201, n. 17.

CONCLUSION

It is only with some hesitation that we have offered this outline of Essene history. It does, however, seem to fit in easily with the main course of Jewish history in the Greco-Roman period. (1) Under Jonathan occurred the secularization of the theocratic power; the 'Essene crisis' was in reality a last effort to maintain the 'splendid isolation' of the Persian and Hellenistic periods. (2) Under John Hyrcanus I and Alexander Jannaeus, Pharisaic influence increased, and after Jannaeus' death the civil authority grew weaker. (3) From Pompey's conquest until the First Jewish Revolt there was a (not unchequered) coexistence of the Pharisaic religious authority with the civil administration in the hands of the last Hasmonaeans and then of the Herodians, the whole being under Roman supervision. (4) After the final incorporation of Judaea into the Roman Empire in 70, and still more so after the crushing of the revolt in 135, the Pharisees alone enjoyed authority in the religious sphere.

So after the days of Jonathan the Essenes were scarcely able to play any part in the political and social life of the Jewish people; they kept themselves separate both physically (by emigrating to Qumrân and later Damascus) and morally (by forming Essene societies living 'in the world'). They merely served as catalysts in each crisis that developed, in religious and political persecutions or in natural disasters. Being born out of an intense ideological crisis and at the moment of a theocratic régime's political bankruptcy, they took a passive part in the internal crises of the Jewish people, although sharing actively in its hopeless uprisings. They form part of the background of more fortunate movements, both ephemeral ones like Gnosticism and more lasting ones like Christianity. But no ancient writer took the trouble to record for posterity the exact nature of the rôle they played in these.

To sum up, the Essenes remained on the outskirts both of the life of the Jewish people, at a time when it was undergoing the rapid transformation that was to result in the stabilization of the form of Judaism that persists until today, and of that of the early Christians in their formative days.

IV

ESSENE ORGANIZATION AND TEACHINGS

THE texts found at Qumrân are our main source of information for reconstructing a picture of the organization and doctrine of the Essenes. Of course, the numerous details preserved for us by Philo and Josephus provide us with important material for comparison.[1]

THE HIERARCHY

Since the sect represented the true Israel, the Israel of the Last Days, it tried to model itself after the pattern of Israel in the days of the Desert Wanderings, described in the Book of Numbers. In the one Israel as in the other the sub-division is first into tribes, then into thousands, hundreds, fifties and tens (cf. 1Q S II. 21 ff., 1Q M passim). But a basic distinction was made between the Sons of Aaron (including the Levites) and the laity (also called generically 'Israel').[2]

The structure of the hierarchy was somewhat complicated. The group of 'camps' in the region of Damascus was provided with two chiefs. One of them, a priest, had the title of 'Priestly inspector of the Many'[3] and the other, a layman, was the 'Superintendent

[1]Philo, *Quod omnis probus liber sit,* 75–91; *Apologia pro Judaeis,* cited *in extenso* by Eusebius, *Praep. Evang.* VIII. 11; Josephus, *War* II. VIII, 119–61, repeated with additional material by Hippolytus in *Elenchus* IX. 18–28; *Ant.* XVIII. 1, 11–22. Mention should also be made of the *De Vita practica, sive de Essenis,* a lost work by Philo, cf. B. Motze, *Atti della R. Accademia delle Scienze di Torino* XLVI, 1910–11, pp. 1–23; J. T. Milik, *Verbum Domini* XXX, 1952, p. 106, n. 1. These accounts of the Essenes and the other two chief Jewish sects most probably have as their common source a lost pamphlet of religious propaganda composed by a Jew of Alexandria towards the start of our era.

[2]There is a tripartite division in 1Q S II. 19–21 (priests, Levites and people) and in VI. 8 f. (priests, elders and the rest of the people), but a quadripartite division in CD XIV. 3–6 (priests, Levites, Israelites and proselytes). Cf. Josephus, *War* II. VIII, 150 (and the expanded version in Hippolytus, *Elenchus* IX. 26) where we find four classes of Essenes, 'according to their seniority in religious life'.

[3]CD XIV. 6 f., and *hakkohen hammupqad 'al harabbim* in unpublished fragments of the *Damascus Document* from Cave IV.

of all the camps' (*hammebaqqer 'ašer lekol hammaḥanot,* CD XIV. 8). The duties of the former were primarily religious, while the latter was especially responsible for the community's property (CD XIV. 13). Each camp had a 'superintendent' (*mebaqqer*) who was also responsible for instructing and guiding candidates for admission; this curious combination of religious and administrative functions is met with again in the *episkopos* of the early Church.[1]

The texts from Qumrân itself are less explicit, although there too we find two titles occurring: the 'Inspector at the head of the Many' (*ha'iš happaqid bero'š harabbim* 1Q S VI. 14) and the 'Superintendent of the Many' (*ha'iš hammebaqqer 'al harabbim* VI. 11 f.) who is probably to be identified with the 'Superintendent of the work of the Many' (VI. 20). However, it is quite possible that at Qumrân there was only one superior official, who was probably a member of the priesthood.

Mention has already been made of camp supervisors, at whose head came the Superintendent General. They were entrusted with various functions and correspond to the *epimeletai* and *epitropoi* of Philo and Josephus.

At Qumrân there was, furthermore, a 'Community Council' composed of twelve laymen and three priests (1Q S VIII. 1 f.). The membership ideally represented the twelve tribes of Israel and the three priestly families, descended from Levi through his three sons Gershon, Kohath and Merari. But in the 'camps' in the land of Damascus we only find a body of ten judges; this is made up of four members of the tribe of Levi (probably three priests and one Levite) and six members representing 'Israel' (CD X. 4 ff.). Rabbinical literature also mentions courts of ten judges, but if we take into account the administrative functions of the court mentioned by the *Damascus Document* (XIV. 13), it is better to compare it with the municipal councils of Hellenistic cities, which also were often composed of ten members, called *deka protoi* ('*ašarta* in the Aramaic section of the Palmyrene *Tariff*).[2]

Some passages (1Q S VI. 3 f.; CD XIII. 2; 1Q 28^a II. 22)

---

[1] The LXX of the Pentateuch translates the roots *pqd* and, more rarely, *bqr* by various forms of *episkopein*. In Hellenistic cultic associations the official responsible for financial matters was called *episkopos* (*TWNT* II, 608, 10).

[2] On the *deko protoi* cf. e.g. Schürer, *Geschichte des Jüdischen Volkes*[4] II, Leipzig 1907, p. 218 (E.T. II. 1, Edinburgh 1898, p. 145); we remember the biblical 'ten rulers that are in a city', Eccles. 7.19.

suggest the existence of 'cells', consisting of ten persons with a priest as president. It will be remembered that the first Christian congregation consisted of about 120 members (Acts 1.15) or ten members to each apostle.[1]

Legislative and juridical authority belonged by right to the Sons of Aaron. Matters that involved both juridical and executive authority, however, were referred to the *mošab harabbim* (the Session of the Many), an assembly where both the Sons of Aaron and the laity had voting rights.[2]

This analysis shows that, though the movement was basically sacerdotal and priests occupied the chief positions in its hierarchy, nevertheless the majority consisted of laymen, as is evident from the expression *harabbim* (literally 'the many'). In addition to this restricted sense, *harabbim* also means the 'general assembly'. This chiefly lay assembly is endowed with considerable juridical powers, and in this we detect a democratic tendency. Both meanings are expressed in the Greek translations of *harabbim*. Josephus uses *pleistoi* for the Essene community as a whole (*Ant.* XVIII. 1, 22) and *pleiones* for the lay members (*War* II. VIII, 146). The New Testament uses both *polloi* and *pleiones*, describing by them the whole congregation—and in contexts often closely parallel to Qumrân texts mentioning *harabbim*. So for instance the last stage of *correptio fraterna* takes place before *pleiones* (II Cor. 2.6) as before *harabbim* (1Q S VI. 1). *Polloi*, as *harabbim*, refers to the whole community as seen in an eschatological context; a striking example is found in the Words of Consecration (Matt. 26.28; Mark 14.24; cf. 'you', Luke 22.20; I Cor. 11.24).

ADMISSION OF NEW MEMBERS

By combining the data of the *Rule* with those provided by Josephus, we can get a clear idea of the stages that candidates had to go through.[3] First of all, they had to spend a year as postulants, during which they tried to live according to the sect's

[1] Cf. Josephus, *War* II. VIII, 146. For the rabbis too the smallest community had to consist of at least ten members (*Megillah* 4.3).

[2] 1Q S VI. 8 ff.; Josephus' 'tribunal' (*War* II, VIII, 145) is clearly identical with this body. From his evidence we know that it consisted of a hundred members; since the basic unit at Qumrân is of ten people (nine plus a priest), this assembly contained ten such units.

[3] 1Q S VI. 13–23 (likewise V. 1 ff., VII. 18–21); cf. *War* II. VIII, 137–9.

rules; they were free to leave at any time. Perhaps this was what happened in the case of the historian Josephus who tells us that he spent three years trying the lives of the three major religious groups, as well as that of a hermit (*Life* II, 10 f.).

The second stage, of novitiate, lasted twice as long, but by the end of the first year the novice was allowed to take part in some of the sect's practices, such as its ritual ablutions. After the completion of the second year, the candidate became a full member of the sect and, among other things, could share in the 'drink of the many' (*mišqeh harabbim*, an expression which is certainly to be interpreted of the sacred meals of the sect, and sometimes is equated with the *ṭohorat harabbim*, the community's practice of purity).

When he attained full membership the novice had to give up the private ownership of his property.[1] Anyone who made a false declaration of his wealth was liable to exclusion from the community 'purity' for a year (1Q S VI. 25; CD XIV. 20). One thinks immediately of the episode of Ananias and Sapphira told in Acts 5.1–11, where a lie in the matter is considered as deserving death in accordance with Ezekiel's teaching that any grave sin in the period of the Last Days would be punished with death (Ezek. 18.4,13). Qumrân law here again shows itself less thoroughly eschatological than that of the New Testament. Moreover, the considerable number of bronze coins found in the remains of the settlement suggests that the members had a certain amount of pocket-money.

There were appropriate ceremonies to mark admission into the postulancy, the novitiate, and especially full membership, but it is difficult to come to a clear picture of how such ceremonies were performed. We are not told whether there were baptismal rites distinct from the daily ablutions of the sect. Accordingly, it is impossible to institute an exact comparison between the ablutions of the Essenes on the one hand, and the baptisms of John the

[1]The hoard of coins found in the ruins of the settlement during the excavations of 1955 contains 550 pieces of silver, minted between the second half of the second century B.C. and the start of the Christian Era. This deposit can be explained, if we suppose that the *mebaqqer* put to one side the money that belonged to the new members of the community at the time when the second period of occupation of the monastery began. For another explanation, cf. *RB* LXIII, 1956, p. 568.

Baptist and of the Christian Church on the other. The *Manual of Discipline* and unpublished fragments of the *Damascus Document* suggest that the main features of the ceremony were the taking of vows and the pronouncing of liturgical formulae of blessing and cursing. The ceremony of initiation ('entering the Covenant') probably took place once a year, at Pentecost, which was for the Essenes the feast of the renewal of the Covenant. Josephus' mention of the 'terrible oaths' that the Essenes had to make seems to refer to this ritual and it is briefly outlined for us, with some verbatim quotations, in the second and fifth columns of the *Manual of Discipline*.

It should be stressed that, inside the community, everyone, priest or layman, had a well-defined rank and there was a wide gap between the lower ranking members and the hierarchy.[1] Perhaps the saying of the Gospel, 'The first will be last and the last first' (Matt. 20.16), belongs to a group of polemical logia directed rather against Essene than Pharisaic practices.[2]

ORA ET LABORA

Legal prescriptions and purificatory rites regulated the Essene's daily life down to the smallest detail. Their time was chiefly given over to manual work to provide for the community's material needs and to worship and the study of the law. The excavations have given us abundant evidence of the manufacturing and agricultural activities of the Essenes, the latter being concentrated round the fresh water springs of 'Ain Fešḫa. Unskilled members probably worked at Fešḫa while the artisans of the community were employed in the workshops at Qumrân itself.[3] The number and the productivity of the copyists at work in the scriptorium would be an unusual feature in comparison with the normal life of a Palestinian rural community.

Their *Officium Divinum* started, as Josephus tells us, early in the morning with the recital of prayers 'received from their forefathers'. This they did facing the rising sun; Josephus' account, which had been misinterpreted as attesting a reverence for the

[1] Cf. Philo, *Quod omnis probus liber sit* 81.

[2] This point of comparison was first suggested by F. M. Cross.

[3] On Essene agricultural and manufacturing activities, cf. Philo, *Quod omnis probus liber sit* 76–78; *Apologia pro Judaeis* 6–9; Josephus, *War* II. VIII, 129, 131; *Ant.* XVIII. I, 19.

rising sun, can in terms of grammar only refer to the direction of their prayer.[1] For other occasions too they observed orientations different from those of the other Jews. The remains of the cultic hall at Qumrân show us a pulpit or lectern at the west, and therefore indicate a westward orientation of the assembly. But in view of their hostile attitude towards the Jerusalem temple of their day, this is probably to be interpreted as a use of the direction adopted by worshippers in the Temple, in which the ark lay to the west, and possibly in the Heavenly Temple also (cf. Ezek. 47.1), rather than a turning towards Jerusalem itself. A further oddity in orientation can be observed in the Qumrân cemetery. The head lay at the south while, according to the orthodox practice of Jews and Christians, it lies to the west. This is probably explained in the light of the Essene belief that Paradise lay to the north and thus at the resurrection the Essene would rise facing it.[2]

Unfortunately, we only have a brief reference in the *Rule* to inform us of the order of their daily gatherings; 'the Many will watch together for a third of every night of the year, to read in the Book, to explain its meaning and to devote their time together to prayer' (VI. 7–8). This regular daily service seems proper to the Qumrân settlement. Philo, in mentioning meetings in the synagogue on the Sabbath during which the Scriptures were read and explained 'allegorically' (*Quod omnis probus liber sit* 81 ff.), is describing the practice of Essenes living in 'the world'. The 'Book' which they read included nearly all of the biblical writings which were shortly afterwards to find a place in the Palestinian Canon, while 'to explain its meaning' should be understood as the application of the hermeneutical principles of the *pešārîm*. As for the 'prayers', the literal translation of the Hebrew word is 'blessings', and several fragmentary manuscripts from Cave IV preserve the text of such blessings as were probably used each day.

Josephus tells us that the Essenes used to put on white clothes for some of their religious services. This is a priestly trait, since the priests of Jerusalem wore white during the Temple service, and one among many such traits that can best be explained if we

[1] Cf. J. Strugnell, *JBL* LXXVII, 1958, pp. 111-13.
[2] J. T. Milik, *RB* LXV, 1958, p. 77.

see in the Essene movement a tendency to make the ritual practices of the priesthood binding on all the community.[1]

THE SACRED BANQUET

As far as the prayers and the reading of the Scriptures were
concerned, the Essene services differed little from the Sabbath
synagogue services of the Roman and Byzantine periods. There
is however one element which distinguishes them, and at the
same time associates them more closely with the services of the
early Christians, the sacred meal.[2]

Essentially, the meal consisted in the taking of bread and wine,
preceded and followed by prayers ('blessings') recited by a priest.
The wine used on these occasions presents a problem. Instead of
the term *yayin*, which one would normally expect, the word
tiroš, properly speaking 'must', is used. Since the Essenes used
tiroš throughout the year, it cannot be meant that they used
grape juice, extracted at the time of the grape picking, which
would by the next July be well fermented, but rather 'sweet wine',
a wine only lightly fermented to prevent it from going bad.

The use of 'sweet wine' is attested in rabbinic literature, where
it is explained that the Nazirite vow is not broken if one drinks
'sweet wine'.[3] This is an important detail, because Eusebius tells

---

[1]For other such practices, cf. *infra*, pp. 106, 114. This 'priesthood of all
believers' is clearly indicated, as J. Strugnell suggests orally, in CD IV. 3 f.

[2]The Essenes' sacred meal is mentioned by Philo (*Quod omnis probus liber
sit* 86; *Apologia pro Judaeis* 11) and described by Josephus (*War* II. VIII,
129–32; *Ant.* XVIII. I, 22; it is priests who prepare their bread). The passage
in *Ant.* XVIII. I, 19 ('they practice sacrifices among themselves') could
refer to their cultic meals, if they considered them as a substitute for the
bloody sacrifices of the Temple. Against Strugnell's different interpretation
of this passage (*JBL* LXXVII, 1958, pp. 113–15) it is significant to note that
there is no trace of an altar at Qumrân—an altar, being of stone, would not
have disappeared. Josephus puts both midday and evening meal on the same
footing as holy meals; the *Rule* does not contradict this, for its prescription
of benedictions in the evening refers to general cultic benedictions and not
specifically to those recited at the sacred meal.

[3]This is deduced *per oppositum* from a text of the Jerusalem Talmud
(*Nedarim* VII. 1): 'A man who has made a vow not to touch *tiroš* is not allowed to touch any "sweet" (drink), but he is allowed to drink ordinary
wine' (cf. *j. Nazir* II. 1). Cf. J. Grinz, *Sinai* XVI, 1952, p. 11–43 (the two
Talmudic passages are cited on p. 15). When Josephus speaks of 'their
continuous sobriety' (*War* II. VIII, 133), he must be referring to their abstention from fully fermented wine.

us that James, 'the brother of the Lord' and first bishop of Jerusalem, was a Nazirite and therefore could not drink fermented wine.[1] It is accordingly permissible to suspect that 'sweet wine' was prescribed for use in Christian liturgical gatherings at Jerusalem. Support for this may be found in a passage in Acts. On the day of Pentecost, the apostles were accused of being 'full of new wine'. The Greek text has *gleukos*, 'sweet wine', which corresponds to the rabbinic term *metîqah*. The incident took place well before the vintage, and so the wine was probably from the preceding year, lightly fermented. Peter's answer does not concern the use of wine, but merely points to the time: 'They are not drunk, as you say, for behold it is only the third hour of the day' (2.15). The implication is that the Eucharist was celebrated in the evening and that 'sweet wine' was used at it.

The Essenes' sacred meals have another characteristic in common with those of the early Christians. One of the Qumrân texts describes the eschatological banquet, and we can see that it is not essentially different from the normal sacred meal.[2] The latter, accordingly, was for the Essenes a foretaste of the banquet to be held in the Last Days. The words of Jesus at the Last Supper express a similar idea: 'I say unto you, I will not eat it (the Passover) again until it is fulfilled in the Kingdom of God . . . for I say unto you, I will not drink of the fruit of the vine, until the Kingdom of God comes' (Luke 22.16–18).

A connexion with the banquets of the mystery religions, which were widespread at that time, or of contemporary pagan religions in general, is not impossible. But the Essenes' sacred meals are essentially a development of those that were held in connexion with the sacrifices prescribed in the Law, where the priest and the faithful who offered a victim entered somehow into intimate relation with God.[3]

On the other hand, there is a great difference between the Essene meal and the Christian Eucharist. The latter brings about a complete union with the Messiah, the Son of God, who gives his servants his body and blood for food. In this respect the

---

[1] *Hist Eccl.* II. xxiii, 5, quoting Hegesippus.
[2] Cf. the first appendix to the *Rule*, 1Q 28ᵃ II. 11–22 (*Discoveries . . .* I, *Rule*, 1Q 28ᵃ II. 11–22, p. 110 f., 117 f.).
[3] Cf. I Cor. 10.18.

Christian is already living in the eschatological era, while the Essene merely has symbols and foretastes of it.

THE CALENDAR AND THE FEASTS

The importance that the Essenes ascribed to the calendar appears from texts like the *Rule* X. 3–8,[1] which alludes vaguely to the various feasts and holy periods and to the duty of observing them. After the discovery of the Qumrân texts it was suggested that the peculiar calendar of Jubilees and I Enoch was followed by the Essenes. This calendar has been studied most recently by Mlle A. Jaubert,[2] who adopted as the starting point of her inquiry a suggestion of D. Barthélemy[3] that the year in this calendar began on Wednesday, the fourth day of the Jewish week.

The year contains 'only 364 days' (Jub. 6.38), a figure divisible by seven; it has twelve months each of thirty days and four intercalary days, one in each period of three months. The three-month period or season contains exactly thirteen weeks (Jub. 6.29), and the days of the week are distributed symmetrically over each period. New Year's day and the first day of each three-month period (1/I, 1/IV, 1/VII, 1/X) always fall on a Wednesday. The dates of the feasts are likewise fixed; a particular day of any given month comes on the same day of the week every year.

Here is their calendar schematically arranged:[4]

Day of the week	I, IV, VII, X	II, V, VIII, XI	III, VI, IX, XII
4th Wed.	1 8 15 22 29	6 13 20 27	4 11 18 25
5th Th.	2 9 16 23 30	7 14 21 28	5 12 19 26
6th Fri.	3 10 17 24	1 8 15 22 29	6 13 20 27
Sabbath	4 11 18 25	2 9 16 23 30	7 14 21 28
1st Sun.	5 12 19 26	3 10 17 24	1 8 15 22 29
2nd Mon.	6 13 20 27	4 11 18 25	2 9 16 23 30
3rd Tues.	7 14 21 28	5 12 19 26	3 10 17 24 31

This reconstruction of the Essene calendar has been substantiated by texts from Cave IV.[5] There is, as has been mentioned, a

[1] Cf. also 1Q H I. 15–20; 1Q S I. 14 f.; CD VI. 18; XVI. 3 f.
[2] *VT* III, 1953, pp. 250–63; *La Date de la Cène*, Études Bibliques, Paris 1957.
[3] *RB* LIX, 1952, pp. 199–203.
[4] Cf. *VT* III, 1953, p. 253; J. Morgenstern's reconstruction of this calendar (*ibid.* V, 1955, p. 60), where the beginning of each three-month period falls on a Tuesday, is unequivocally excluded by Cave IV texts.
[5] See Additional Note 5.

group of manuscripts which deal with the rotation of duty for the priestly families in the Temple. The pattern of the work is simple; a typical sentence is as follows: 'The 16th of the same (month, i.e. the second month of the first year) is the Sabbath of Melakiah.' This means that Melakiah would have begun his week of duty in the Temple on the Sabbath, the 16th of the second month. The priestly roster is spread over six years, and this sexennial cycle reflects a desire to synchronize the sect's religious calendar (of twelve months with thirty days each and four intercalated days, i.e. a solar reckoning) with the luni-solar calendar (of twelve months with alternatively twenty-nine and thirty days and a month intercalated every three years). According to the calculations of the Qumran scribes, the two calendars synchronize every three years ($364 \times 3 = 354 \times 3 + 30$). Six years are needed for a priestly family's turn to come round again in the same week of the year, since there were twenty-four families (cf. I Chron. 24.7–18) serving thirteen times in such a period ($24 \times 13 = 52 \times 6$). A work from Qumrân, preserved in three copies, gives this triple synchronism of the religious calendar, the luni-solar calendar and the weekly roster of the priests. For example, 'Friday in Yeḥezq'el, the 29th (day)—the 22nd of the eleventh month', is to be understood as follows: 'The 22nd day of the eleventh month (of the first year in the religious calendar) falling on the Friday in the week when Yeḥezq'el is on duty, corresponds to the 29th (and last) day of the eleventh month (Šebṭ) in the luni-solar calendar.'[1]

The same work also gives a list of feasts, together with the priestly family on duty at that time. For instance, 'The first year, its feasts. Tuesday (i.e. the evening of the 14th day of the first month) in (the week of) Me'ozyah: Passover. Sunday (the 26th of the first month) in (the week of) Yeda'yah: Waving of the First Sheaf'. The Essene festival cycle contained seven principal feasts. It started with Passover on the evening of the 14th of the first month, and after this came the Octave of the Feast of Unleavened Bread. The Offering of the First Sheaf (also called the

---

[1]Other manuscripts from Cave IV attempt to synchronize the Essene six-year cycle with the biblical cycle of sabbatical and lunar periods. Further, they give dates according to the solar calendar for the experimentally observed phases of the moon.

Barley Festival), which was to be made on 'the morrow of the Sabbath' (Lev. 23.15 f.), was fixed for the 26th of the first month, or on the Sunday after the Sabbath following the Octave of Passover.[1] The Second Passover, prescribed in the Bible for those unable to keep the normal Passover in Jerusalem (Num. 9.9–12), fell before the Feast of Weeks, a month after the First Passover (on Thursday, the evening of the 14th day in the second month). In the Pharisaic calendar *Megillat Ta'anit*, it is called the Little Passover and falls likewise a month after the first. Fifty days after the Barley Festival, on the 15th of the third month, falls the Feast of Weeks (cf. Jub. 15.1; 16.12 f.; 44.1–5); as the Feast of the Renewal of the Covenant, this seems to have been the Essenes' most important festival (cf. the following section).

The cycle of autumnal feasts began with the New Year (1/VII). Interestingly, this is not only called *ro'š haššanah* ('the beginning of the year') but also *yom bazzikaron* ('the Day of Commemoration'). On the tenth day of the same month, therefore a Friday, fell the Day of Atonement, and on Wednesday the 15th of the seventh month, the Feast of Tabernacles.

As well as these traditional feast-days and the regular series of Sabbaths and New-moons, there were some extra holidays. The day after each of the four intercalary days, i.e. the first of each new season, is called a 'Day of Commemoration' in Jub. 6.23. It is quite possible to see these feasts in the list in 1Q S X. 7: 'the Feast of Harvest, the Feast of Summer Fruits, the Feast of Sowing, the Feast of Spring Shoots'. These accordingly fell on 1/I, 1/IV, 1/VII, 1/X. A fragment from the fourth Cave also mentions the 'Feast of Oil', which fell on the 22nd day of the sixth month. As can be seen from the names, these feasts are connected with the agricultural year. Futhermore, in some of the calendars historical events are commemorated in the same

---

[1] The Pharisees held that by 'the morrow of the Sabbath' the day after Passover was meant (16th Nisan), Passover being reckoned as a Sabbath because it was a day of rest. But the Boethusians, traditionally identified with the Sadducees, and the Samaritans interpreted the scriptural phrase to mean the day after a 'real' Sabbath. The latter group takes this as the Sabbath inside the Passover Octave. It has been occasionally proposed to identify the Boethusians with the Essenes; so e.g. Azariah dei Rossi (*Me'or Enayîm*, sixteenth century), Kohut, Grinz (*Sinai* XVI, 1952, pp. 11–43) who interpret their name as *bet* + *'Essaya* (*vel sim.*), 'the school of the Essenes'.

way that we find them in I Maccabees and in the Tractate *Ta'anit*.[1]

The calendar used by the authors of Jubilees and I Enoch and by the settlers at Qumrân and by the camps of the Land of Damascus presents two problems: Where did it originate? How was it synchronized with the astronomical year?

The Qumrân texts give us no material for solving the second problem, viz., what was done about the extra one and a quarter days, the approximate difference between a year of 364 days and the astronomical year of 365.2422 days. Hypothetically, given the triennial and sexennial cycles mentioned above, a twenty-four year cycle would have to be established; after four sexennial cycles, a month of 29 (or to be more precise, 29.76) days would have to be intercalated. In this way, the 364-day year would be harmonized with the phases of the moon. But such an additional month would have required an additional turn of duty from four priestly families every twenty-four years. To make each of the 24 families take part in this duty, a cycle of 144 years (24 × 6) would be necessary.

The problem of the origins of this system is more obscure. Mlle Jaubert has made it highly probable that this calendar was used by the latest redactors of the Pentateuch, by Ezekiel, and by the Chronicler.[2] It is known, therefore, at least as far back as the Exile, although this does not prove that it was actually in use in the Temple at that time. Against such an assumption we should note that the twenty-four family service prescribed for the restored Temple presupposes a luni-solar calendar rather than a solar calendar of fifty-two weeks. But it may have been used at an earlier date—perhaps not as the only calendar but as the one regulative of cultic life. In Egypt, too, different calendars were followed for political and religious purposes. Indeed, this old religious Israelite calendar followed closely the Egyptian religious calendar where the year consisted of twelve months, each of thirty days, and five intercalated days. There is no reason why one should not suppose that it was borrowed from Egypt

---

[1] Cf. J. T. Milik, *VT* Suppl. IV, 1957, pp. 24–26.

[2] Some striking examples may be cited. The flood lasted exactly one solar year; Enoch lived 365 years. If we interpret the dates of the events in the Patriarchs' lives according to the Essene calendar, we attain the satisfactory result that they never go on a journey on the Sabbath—a result unlikely to be fortuitous.

hrough the Phoenicians at the beginning of the Israelite monarchy. Slightly changed from its Egyptian model after the Exile
e.g. the division into four seasons, whereas the Egyptians had
only three, and the reduction of intercalary days from five to four),
his calendar could have remained in use in the Temple until
he Hellenistic period. In civil life, however, from the Persian
period onward the lunisolar calendar (of Babylonian origin)
was employed. It can be imagined that at some time an attempt
was made to introduce this calendar (in the form known as
'Seleucid') into the Temple as well. The priesthood of Jerusalem
would have supported or opposed this change according to their
attitude towards Hellenism. The author of Daniel seems to allude
to such a controversy when he accuses Antiochus IV Epiphanes
of having sought to change 'the times and the law' (Dan. 7.25).
The Book of Jubilees, with its polemic against the lunar calendar
and its stubborn defence of the traditional one—attitudes found
also in the Qumrân texts—may well have been composed shortly
after the suppression of the traditional calendar in the Temple
services. Might it not have been Jonathan himself, in his desire
to integrate his country with the political and cultural life of the
Hellenistic world, who took such a drastic step? And might not
this have been one of the reasons, if not the main one, for the
exodus of the Essenes?

Some observations, however, on this theory are not out of
place. As far as concerns the actual use of this calendar in the
First and Second Temples, the evidence of biblical texts only
gives us a *non liquet*, with perhaps a slight tendency to favour its
use. The calendar question, as we see from the Qumrân writings,
provides a thoroughly satisfactory reason for the Essene schism.
But only the fact that such a calendar *had been in use* before, and
was later dropped, would have sufficed to cause a schism. Accordingly we must either extend our *non liquet* from this calendar's
cultic use to its being the reason for the Essene schism, or else,
accepting this reason, accept with it that the calendar was at some
time actually followed in the Temple service. Such a calendar
was certainly followed by the Essenes in their cultic life—and
the *Mišmarôt* from Cave IV confirm thoroughly the Barthélemy–
Jaubert reconstruction of its form. Its use and defence by the
Essenes would be yet another instance of how their law and

practices were more conservative than those of the Pharisees.

We may mention an interesting consequence that Mlle Jaubert proposes to derive from this calendar, namely, that the Last Supper was celebrated by Jesus as the Essene Passover on the Tuesday evening in Holy Week.[1] In this way she resolves the contradiction between the Synoptic Gospels, in which the Last Supper is a Passover meal, and the Gospel of St John, in which the Passover starts on the Friday evening, Jesus being crucified as the Passover Offering. This suggestion also provides a more leisurely sequence of events for the various trials of Jesus.

Our first observation about this suggestion concerns *method*. It is certain that in some early Christian groups the Last Supper was commemorated on a Tuesday evening; it is true also that Tuesday evening is the beginning of the Passover in the Essene calendar. But it does not follow that the Judaeo-Christian practice indicates a survival of the Essene calendar among them; other *liturgical* causes may likewise be suspected. To go further and to assume a historical cause in the life of Jesus for a late liturgical practice is even more questionable. The same is true of the attempt to reconcile one out of numerous discrepancies between two literary sources, the Synoptics and St John, by an appeal to conjectural historical fact.

But even on the basis of *historical* fact, objection can be raised. Mlle Jaubert's theory presupposes that the Essene Passover, on Wednesday of the solar calendar, fell also on the Wednesday preceding a Saturday Passover according to the official calendar. We have, therefore, to assume that the feast fell in the same week in the two calendars. Such a coincidence would happen about once in thirty years. Secondly, we cannot assume that Jesus and his disciples celebrated the Passover according to a sectarian calendar, without considering the consequences that this will have on our understanding of his reported observance of other Jewish festivals (e.g. Tabernacles, and especially Encaenia which is not mentioned in Essene writings). Are not Christ and his disciples reported regularly as keeping the feasts according to the orthodox calendar, making pilgrimages to Jerusalem at the times prescribed in the Law, mingling and speaking with the vast

[1]Cf. A. Jaubert, *La Date de la Cène*, and E. Vogt, *Biblica* XXXVI, 1955, pp. 408 ff.

rowds who did likewise? And the evangelists often stress Jesus' respect for the Temple as it functioned, and acknowledgment of the validity of the priesthood of his day (Matt. 8.4; cf. 3.2–3). Since we cannot assume that Christ followed one calendar on one occasion and another on another (the use of a given calendar being a *decisive* criterion of religious affiliation), this well attested observance of the common calendar and loyalty towards the constituted religious authorities, renders impossible a hypothesis which would make Jesus and his disciples for all practical purposes Essenes.

If these historical objections be neglected and the hypothesis be accepted, we have, it is true, economy of explanation—many perplexing phenomena of different orders are explained by one hypothesis. But while a historical event cannot be excluded *a priori* as a cause for liturgical and literary phenomena, it is often far from being the most plausible, especially if it leaves unexplained other facets of what we have hitherto regarded as the same literary or liturgical problem.[1]

THE TRUE ISRAEL AND THE NEW COVENANT

The Essenes' teachings on God, the world and Man do not differ substantially from the Old Testament doctrine; they merely develop it. The devoted long reflection to the key biblical idea that while many of the Chosen People fell by the wayside, God would continue to work his saving plan upon an ever-diminishing number of the people, until the last days when those left would be the 'Remnant of Israel' *par excellence*.[2] Stirred by the conviction that the end was at hand, and that they themselves were God's chosen 'Remnant', the followers of the Teacher united together to follow a common way of life and a strict rule. Their relations with God were founded on the 'New Covenant' which Jeremiah had proclaimed (31.31–4, cf. Ezek. 36.22–8). This phrase (*habberît haḥadašah*)[3] and similar ones run through the whole of the *Damascus Document*.

The renewed covenant was confirmed by a special revelation granted to the Teacher of Righteousness. He was given an under-

---

[1] For a similar critique, cf. P. Benoit's review of Mlle Jaubert's book in *RB* LXV, Oct. 1958.

[2] Cf. CD I–VIII, XIX–XX.

[3] CD VIII. 21 (=XIX. 33); XX. 12; perhaps 1Q pHab II. 3.

standing of God's promises that exceeded even that of the inspired writers themselves. 'God told Habakkuk to write out all that would come to pass in the last generation, but he did not grant him to know the time when these things would come to pass . . . Its meaning refers to the Teacher of Righteousness, to whom God made known all the mysteries of the words (spoken by) his servants, the prophets' (pHab VII. 1–2, 4–5; cf. II. 5–10). This knowledge is, accordingly, apocalyptic, and the expectation of 'the End of Days' leaves its mark on every facet of the lives of members of the New Covenant. During this period which precedes the End of Times, the laws observed have only a provisional and temporary value (1Q S IX. 10 f.; CD XIV. 18 f.). Later on they will be replaced by a new and final Law, proclaimed by the eschatological figure called 'the Interpreter of the Law'.

There is, however, one noteworthy difference between the teaching of the Old Testament and that of the sect. To belong to the Covenant the candidate must not only be a member of the Chosen People; a free act of choice is also necessary.[1] This is it is true, subject to certain limitations. In addition to the hierarchy's power of veto and its right to exclude candidates, certain physical or moral defects were considered diriment impediments. An unpublished manuscript of the *Damascus Document*, whose fragments were found in Cave IV (provisional abbreviation 4Q D*b*), enables us to fill in the lacunae in the corresponding section of the Cairo Manuscript (XV. 15–17): 'Fools, madmen (*mšwg‘*), simpletons and imbeciles (*mšwgh*), the blind (*lit.*, those who, being weak of eye, cannot see), the maimed (*ḥgr*), the lame, the deaf, and minors, none of these may enter the midst of the community, for the holy angels (are in the midst of it).'

We find a similar list in the first appendix to the *Rule*, but there it occurs in connexion with the future 'congregation' and not with the present one on earth.[2] It is to be stressed that these lists of defects are expansions of the lists of priestly disqualifications found in the Pentateuch—another example of how the Essenes universalized regulations once proper to the priesthood alone

[1] For the expression, 'those who have volunteered for the Law' (1Q S V. 1 etc.), cf. I Macc. 2.42 (*pas ho hekousiazomenos tô nomô* of the Asideans). Philo too, notes that the system of application for membership implies the candidate's free decision (*Apologia pro Judaeis* 2).

[2] 1Q 28*a* II. 3–9 (*Discoveries* . . . I, pp. 110, 116); cf. also 1Q M VII. 3–6

One immediately thinks of the Gospel parable of the invitation to the banquet as St Luke records it. 'The poor, the maimed, the blind and the lame' are summoned to take the place of the original guests 'at the feast in the Kingdom of God' (14.15–21). Perhaps here, too, we have a polemical reference to Essene belief.

In any case, this exclusiveness helped to give the sect its closed and esoteric character. Josephus tells us that candidates for membership had to swear not to give away the secrets which they had been taught, even though they were tortured to death.[1] A further confirmation of this esoteric character comes in the use of cryptic devices for copying books considered to be particularly important. Two different alphabets have been found, where arbitrarily chosen signs are substituted for all the letters of the Hebrew alphabet. Even more naïve is the case in another manuscript where the writing runs from left to right and normal characters are occasionally replaced by their Greek or Phoenician equivalents. The use of cryptic alphabets seems to be found mainly in the earliest period of Essene copying activity, and perhaps their declining popularity can be associated with the slackening of sectarian consciousness that we have detected elsewhere.

In the Old Testament we see how God used mediators for concluding or renewing his Covenant. The Teacher of Righteousness is a sort of mediator of the New Covenant, but only in that he explained how the New Covenant would operate. As was said above, the Essenes were called basically to repeat the experience of their forefathers who had lived forty years in the desert, while overcoming the trials through which that generation had failed to come successfully. Once again, we find a parallel in the Gospel accounts of Jesus' temptations in the wilderness, of which Mark (1.13, cf. Luke 4.1–13) gives a schematized version and Matthew (4.1–11) a longer one. There Jesus is shown triumphing over temptations similar to those experienced after the Exodus (cf. Deut. 8.3; 6.13–16); he thus inaugurates the eschatological era which includes a return to the conditions of life that obtained at the beginning in Paradise. 'Jesus was with wild animals and angels served him' (Mark 1.13).

When the Essenes first established themselves in the Wilderness

---

[1] *War* II. VIII, 141; cf. 1Q S IX. 17, 22; X. 24 (the uncorrected text) and also VIII. 18; CD XV. 10 f.

of Judaea, they predicted a forty years' period for their stay, showing that they conceived this time as parallel to the Desert Sojourn of the Hebrews. In this light they interpreted Isa. 40.3: 'The voice of one crying: In the wilderness prepare ye the way of the Lord, make straight in the desert a highway for our God' (cf. 1Q S VIII. 15 f.; IX. 19 ff.), as commanding a separation from wicked men, and a life in the desert studying and practising the Law according to its true meaning which had been revealed to them. If their community were to live such a life, they would be preparing 'a highway for our God'. The *Damascus Document*[1] also foresaw a period of forty years, which in this case is dated from the death of the Teacher of Righteousness. If during these forty years the whole community kept the Covenant, God would annihilate the impious ones of Israel. In contrast to the idea in the *Rule,* where their holy way of life almost automatically brought about God's coming at the end, the vision here is more diversified. There is emphasis on the judgement of the wicked; the Essenes by their holy lives condemn and bring judgement upon them, and this during the period of forty years, not merely at its end.

Thus in the early days of the Qumrân settlement the importance of the holy living of the community for bringing judgement to pass was never obscured. But towards the end, as the idea of the Final War which would eliminate all iniquity gained in vividness, less attention was paid to this aspect. In the Final War (cf. 1Q M II. 6 f.) which again would last for forty years, it is not enough that by their holy living they are preparing for the coming of the Kingdom of God. They must participate actively on the side of God and his angels, in the struggles as well as in the judgement.

Their way of life included the daily scrupulous observance of a set of social and religious rules which left nothing to chance. Entry into the sect took on a special importance; it took place on the day of the Feast of the Renewal of the Covenant, which is described in the *Rule* (I. 7–II. 19). It consisted of prayers of thanksgiving and of praise, a short form of public confession, and, most important, a blessing on the 'Men of God's lot' together with a double curse upon the 'Men of Belial's lot', which is reminiscent of the famous ceremony prescribed by Moses to

[1] XX. 13 ff.; cf. 4Q pPs 37.10 (*PEQ* 1954, p. 69 ff.).

take place on Mount Gerizim and Mount Ebal (Deut. 27.11–26). At this festival, probably, Essenes from the most distant communities gathered together at the mother-house at Qumrân; it is tempting to associate with this feast the abundant animal bones (of sheep, goats and cattle) which are certainly the remains of meals, and were found in association with a large number of vases during the excavations.

The date of this commemoration of the giving of the Covenant is of some significance. In the Old Testament, no precise date is given for the arrival at Sinai and Moses' ascent of the mountain. Ex. 19.1 only says: 'In the third month after their departure from the land of Egypt, on this day [*sic!*] the children of Israel came to the desert of Sinai . . . and Moses went up the mountain to God.' Later Jewish tradition was divided, some placing this event on the first of the month, but the majority on the Feast of Weeks.[1] My Samaritan informants tell me that they believe that the revelation on Mount Sinai took place at the Feast of Pentecost. As far as the Essenes are concerned the evidence is quite clear. Our oldest manuscript of the *Damascus Document* places the ceremony of the renewal of the Covenant in the third month of the year. The Book of Jubilees makes its dating on the fifteenth day of that month certain. Although the covenant with Noah is not dated formally, its connexion with Pentecost is explicit. As the author says (6.17 f.): 'For this reason it is ordained and written on the heavenly tablets that they should celebrate the Feast of Weeks in this month once a year to renew the Covenant once a year. And this whole festival was celebrated in heaven from the days of Creation till the days of Noah . . . and from the day of Noah's death, his sons did away with it till the days of Abraham . . . but Abraham observed it and Isaac and Jacob observed it up to thy days, and in thy days the children of Israel forgot it until ye celebrated it anew on this mountain.' The Covenant of Abraham is explicitly put at the middle, i.e. fifteenth, of the third month (14.14–20). Other important events took place on the same day of the year, such as the meeting of the three patriarchs in Beersheba (22.1–7), the covenant of Jacob and Laban (29.7), the vision of Jacob before his descent into Egypt (44.5), and most important (and linked by the author

[1] *Exodus Rabba ad loc., b Šab.* 88*ᵃ*, *b Pes.* 68*ᵇ*.

117

with the earlier covenants with Noah and Abraham) the Covenant at Sinai; this took place, it is implied, during the Feast (cf. Jub. 6.19 *supra*) and was followed by the forty days of instruction which began on the sixteenth day of the third month. For the early Christians, too, the New Covenant was confirmed on the same Day of Pentecost, although in this case it was no longer reserved to the twelve tribes but offered to all the languages of the world.

THE TWO SPIRITS

Life in conformity with the New Covenant has a double character: on the one hand, there is a struggle for the coming of the Last Times; on the other, a foretaste of the enjoyment of the blessed life that these times inaugurate. The forces of Good and those of Evil are struggling with each other for power over the present world, and are in conflict even within the heart of man. On one side stands *Belial,* the *Angel of Darkness*, with his hosts, the *Spirits of Wickedness* or *Spirits of Darkness*. On the other is the *Prince of Light* with his forces, the *Spirits of Truth* or *Spirits of Light* (cf. 1Q S III. 13–IV. 1).[1] A psychological expression of this cosmic dualism is found in the catalogue of virtues and vices, in 1Q S IV. 2–14.[2]

The doctrine of the two spirits was, it is well known, one of the favourite themes of the Jewish-Christians. The section of the *Didache* called 'The Two Ways' seems to be almost a translation of part of the *Rule* (III. 13–IV. 1) and it was repeated almost verbatim by the *Epistle of Barnabas*.[3]

Although dualist, the Essenes' doctrine of the world and the human soul does not go beyond the limits of biblical monotheism; it is God who will bring about the final victory of Good over Evil. Although a Persian influence can be detected, orthodoxy remains safe.

[1]Cf. 'Spirit of Truth and Spirit of Error', I John 4.6 (and *Test. Judah* 20.1). 'The Spirit of Light' occurs in CD V. 18, in opposition to Belial; cf. 'the Angel of Light' in II Cor. 11.14 (opposed to Satan).

[2]On the Essenes' practice of virtue, cf. Philo, *Quod omnis probus liber sit* 83 f.; Josephus, *War* II. VIII, 139–42. For catalogues of virtues in St Paul, cf. Gal. 5.19–23; Eph. 4.25–5.13; I Cor. 6.9 f.; Col. 3.5–9. The existence of a thoroughly Jewish source for these catalogues makes it unnecessary to assume *direct* borrowing from Hellenistic models.

[3]*Didache* I. 1 ff.; *Doctrina Apostolorum* I. 1–VI. 5; *Epistle of Barnabas* XVIII–XX. Cf. J. P. Audet, *RB* LIX, 1952, pp. 219–38.

A similar judgement has to be given on the doctrine of divine transcendence. The Essenes had a keen sense of this, even to the extent that their picture of the physical and spiritual world was coloured by a marked determinism.[1] Under the influence of certain astrological theories, current at the time, they held that human life and activity was strictly regulated by the movements of the heavenly bodies which themselves were ruled by angels, as the Book of Enoch insists. Furthermore, on the psychological level, man was the plaything of the opposed forces of Good and Evil, which were striving each to possess him. A work from Cave IV provides us with an interesting example of this double (physical and psychic) determinism. It teaches the physical characteristics of people born under a given sign of the Zodiac, and the exact proportion of their share in the world of the Spirits of Light, and in that of the Spirits of Darkness. When Josephus mentions their belief in *heimarmene*,[2] he is translating this belief into Greek terms. However, with the insouciance for logical niceties characteristic of Semitic theologies, man will still be punished for his sinful acts.

THE SPIRITUAL LIFE OF THE ESSENES

We should first note how certain passages of the Essene texts bear witness to a fine moral sense. For instance, in the section of the *Rule* which deals with the confession of sins (X. 16–25) we find words that are close to the spirit of the Sermon on the Mount: 'I render unto no man evil for evil: with good I try to reach him' (*ibid.* 17 f.). Charity is the basis of human relationships. The *Damascus Document* lays down that 'to the poor and the wretched, to the old and infirm, to the unfortunate, to those who are captives in a foreign land, spinsters (*lit.* 'virgins without a protector'), to orphaned children ('with none to take care of them') and to every one of the brethren whose house in one way or another is threatened with danger', the community should show sympathy and set aside for them part of its income (CD XIV. 14–17, corrected and supplemented on the basis of unpublished fragments from Qumrân IV).[3] It is interesting to note how

[1] Cf. e.g. 1Q H I. 23–5, 27–9; VII. 28 ff.; IX. 16 f.; X. 1 ff.; XII. 10 f
[2] *Ant.* XIII. v, 172; XVIII. 1, 18.
[3] On the Essenes' private practice of charity, cf. *War* II. VIII, 134. The sick and old were supported from the community chest (Philo, *Quod omnis probus liber sit* 87; *Apologia pro Judaeis* 13).

the community's almsgiving, like their sharing of property, which, in Christianity, remained a voluntary personal practice, here became a communal institution; the Essenes were a much closer anticipation of the modern welfare state than the Christians.

Reference has been made to the lofty idea current among the Essenes concerning God's power and holiness. They realized, moreover, man's congenital inability to carry out his part in God's plan of salvation. A passage in the *Hymns* declares:

> What then is this flesh, what is this creature of clay
> That he should show forth the greatness of thy marvels?
> He who lay in iniquity since his mother's womb,
> And until old age abides in sin and disobedience!
> I know that righteousness belongs not to man,
> Nor perfection of conduct to the son of man.
> To God most High belongs every righteous work,
> Man's conduct will not stand firm,
> Unless God fashion his spirit in him;
> He alone can make perfect the paths of the son of man,
> So that all creatures may know the might of his power,
> And the greatness of his mercy upon all his sons in whom he
>   is well pleased . . .
> I have said: 'Because of my faithlessness I was left out of
>   thy Covenant';
> But then remembering the might of thy right hand, and the
>   abundance of thy mercies,
> I *arose* and stood upright,
> And my spirit stood its ground in the face of ill-fortune.
> I have leaned on thy goodness, and on the abundance of thy
>   mercies.
> Yea, thou pardonest iniquity,
> And in thy righteousness thou purifiest man from sin (1Q H
>   IV. 29–33, 35–8).

The Essenes realized that they were living in a transitional period, that was dominated by the battle between Good and Evil. This did not, however, prevent them from experiencing real joy, based on the certainty that their way of life put them in a most intimate contact with God and the Spirits of Good. Another passage from the *Hymns* runs as follows:

I thank thee, O Lord,
For thou hast redeemed my soul from the Pit,
From Hell's perdition thou hast caused me to rise up to the
    everlasting heights,
And I walk over an endless plain.
I have realised that for thy creature, whom thou hast formed
    out of clay,
There is hope that he will join in thy everlasting council.
The broken spirit thou hast cleansed of his great faithlessness,
So that he should stand in thy service, in his rank in the army
    of the Holy Ones,
And should enter into fellowship with the company of the
    Sons of Heaven;
Thou hast cast the lot for him, that he should stand forever
    among the Spirits of Knowledge,
So that he should praise thy name amid the rejoicings of the
    congregation,
And tell forth thy wonders to all thy creatures (1Q H
    III. 19–23).

This motive of living in fellowship with the angels, is not
merely a lyrical expression; it occurs also in legal texts as a reason
for certain purity regulations—a development of the recurrent
phrase in Leviticus: 'Ye shall be holy, for I Yahweh am holy.'[1]

THE ESCHATOLOGICAL WAR

Although each day's life was a struggle between the forces of
good and evil, the Essenes kept their gaze fixed on the final
battle, which would mark the crisis at the end of days. Their
main interests were in the moral and human aspects of this
conflict; in contrast with the author of the Book of Enoch, they
did not become fascinated by its cosmic character. They knew of
the belief that the universe would finally dissolve in a great conflagration (cf. 1Q H III. 28–36),[2] but they gave man a part to
play in the pain and travail out of which a new world would be

---

[1] Cf. CD XV. 15–17 already cited; 1Q 28ª II. 8f. and also I Cor. 11.10; Matt.
18.10; and Strugnell's discussion of Josephus, *War* II. VIII, 148, in *JBL*
LXXVII, 1958, p. 113, n. 30.
[2] The belief of the Essenes in a universal conflagration is referred to by
Hippolytus, *Elenchus* IX. 27.

born. To describe it, they use terms and images drawn from child-birth, and also the symbol of a boat tossed about by a hurricane (1Q H III. 1–18).

The final struggle was to be a war of extermination, in which the certainty that the Sons of Light would triumph over the Sons of Darkness did not in any way exempt them from employing all their efforts in the conflict.

The Sons of Light seem to have been made up of two groups; first, 'the Sons of Levi, Judah and Benjamin', called also 'the exiled in the Wilderness' (i.e. the Wilderness of Qumrân and Judaea in general); and secondly, 'the Sons of Light exiled in the Wilderness of the Nations' (i.e. in the camps in the land of Damascus and in the Diaspora generally), who will return to take part in the eschatological war to be waged in the 'Desert of Jerusalem' (1Q M I. 2 f.). It is interesting to note that this last place name is also found in monastic writings of the Byzantine period.[1]

A manual entitled *The Rule for the War* provides instructions to ensure the triumph of the Forces of Light (Plate 17). It appears from this book that the eschatological era will come in after forty years; this period is subdivided in the following way: there are six years of preparation for war, followed by twenty-nine years of campaigns against the various foreign nations, one after the other; but every seventh year is devoted to rest, and military activity is suspended (1Q M II. 8 ff.).

At the head of the side of the righteous stand two messianic leaders: the High Priest (*hakkohen haro'š*) and the Prince of the Congregation (*nesi' ha'edah*).

We have already proposed in chapter II a literary genesis for *The Rule for the War* and noted how the military details in it suggest dependence on a military manual composed during Herod's reign. The *Rule* was composed after this manual, and shortly after the death of Herod, at a time when tension between Jews and the Roman authorities was mounting and on the way to burst into explosion in the First Jewish Revolt. The notion of a march of the Forces of Light, led by the Messiah, from the 'Desert of the Nations' to do battle before the walls of

---

[1]See the letter quoted by E. Schwartz, *Kyrillos von Skythopolis* (Texte und Untersuchungen 49.2, 1939), p. 391, n. 1; John Moschus, *Pratum Spirituale* 92, 105 (*PG* LXXXVII, 2949, 2961).

Jerusalem occurs also in the *pešārîm*. Beneath the walls of the Holy City he will give battle to the troops of the Kittiim who will arrive from the plain of Acre. This apocalyptic march of the Roman army is prefigured, in the eyes of the author of the *Commentary on Isaiah*, by the route of the Syrian invader, described in Isaiah.[1] The idea of a march from the desert to face the Forces of Iniquity is not specifically Essene. Josephus mentions several agitators whose actions become much more understandable to us now we can read the *Rule for the War*. One such was an Egyptian in the time of the procuratorship of Felix. Calling himself a prophet, he gathered together 4,000 *sicarii* in the desert of Jerusalem (Acts 21.38) and marched to the Mount of Olives where the Roman legionaries dispersed them easily.[2] These *sicarii* are not necessarily Essenes, but the schema that they follow is analogous.

One would not be surprised to find that the leaders of the Jewish Revolt had considered the *Rule for the War* as an excellent piece of propaganda, nor that at the signal for the outburst of the Revolt the Essenes left Qumrân, after hiding their manuscripts away in caves, and joined the ranks of those who were fighting the Romans (the Kittiim of our texts), who were the 'Sons of Belial' *par excellence*.[3] This Holy War was doomed to pitiful failure and the Essenes' strictest group never returned to Qumrân. Whether, where and for how long the community survived, we cannot say.

THE TWO MESSIAHS

The period of the end will be brought in by God. On this point Essene belief is at one with the Old Testament. But on God's agents in bringing in his Kingdom their teaching is far more complicated. The evolution of their belief in the Messiah or Messiahs is hard to trace; especially its character at the beginning is unknown to us, since the relevant section in the *Rule* (1Q S IX. 10 f.) does not occur in the oldest manuscript (4Q S^e) of the work. This copies 1Q S IX. 12 directly after VIII. 16. It is accordingly probable that a later addition was made, although the shorter redaction leaves the impression of abruptness and may

[1] 10.27–32, cf. *JBL* LXXV, 1956, p. 178.
[2] Cf. F. M. Abel, *Histoire de la Palestine*, Paris 1952, I, p. 465.
[3] Josephus mentions that the Essenes were persecuted during the 'war against the Romans', *War* II. VIII, 152 f.

represent an intermediate stage between the original text and that found in 1Q S.

For the first half of the first century we have a wealth of evidence about Qumrân messianism, in the manuscript of the *Rule* from the first cave together with its appendices as well as the *Testimonia* document and the earliest copy of the *Damascus Document* (4Q D*ᵇ*). In the manuscript of the *Rule* it is stated that the laws that the community observes will be valid 'until the advent of the Prophet and of the Messiahs of Aaron and of Israel' (1Q S IX. 11). However this belief developed later, it is clear that the copyist of this document thought of three persons; grammatically this is the only possible interpretation. The same belief in two Messiahs, although their titles are slightly different, is found in the same scribe's copy of one of the appendices to the *Rule,* the *Serek Ha ʿedah.* In this text the eschatological banquet is presided over by *hakkohen,* 'the Priest' *par excellence* (1Q 28*ᵃ* II. 19) and the Messiah of Israel (*ibid.* 14, 20). In the second appendix, containing Benedictions, there is a very fragmentary Benediction for the Priestly Messiah; although the title and most of the text is missing, his liturgical functions are stressed in what remains. There is another far better preserved blessing for the Royal Messiah, the 'Prince (*nasî*') of the Whole Congregation'; this title is derived from Ezekiel's Davidic *nasî*' (34.24; 37.25). In it he appears as one who will dispense justice to his people and through successful campaigns establish Israelite domination over all nations.

There is a striking illustration of this phase of Essene messianic doctrine in the 4Q *Testimonia* document, a *florilegium* of quotations copied *c*. 100 B.C. and almost completely preserved. The scribe quoted first three texts from the Pentateuch: first of all, Deut. 18.18 ff., 'I will raise up from among you a Prophet . . .', combined with 5.28 ff. Next comes Balaam's oracle on the star of Jacob, Num. 24.15–17, and finally Jacob's blessing on Levi, from Deut. 33.8–11.[1] Surprisingly enough, these three biblical passages

---

[1]This document was first published by J. M. Allegro, *JBL* LXXV, 1956, pp. 182–87. To be more precise, the first combined text is quoted word for word according to the Samaritan recension in which it is found inserted in Ex. 20.21b, with the same introductory formula. This observation of Skehan (*Catholic Biblical Quarterly* XIX, 1957, p. 435) shows that the texts were cited in the order of their occurrence in the Bible.

concerning the Messiahs of the future are followed by a quotation from a non-biblical book, the pseudepigraphical *Psalms of Joshua*, containing an allusion to events in the past and connected with the persecutors of the sect. In virtue of its context we have to assume that these events too had an eschatological significance. Probably, we should see here a parallel to the early Christian belief that the activity of a person considered to be Antichrist is a sure indication that the kingdom of God is at hand; the persecutions of the elect are the birth-pangs of the messianic age.[1]

By their choice of passages from the Pentateuch, the Scriptures *par excellence*, the Essenes supported their own belief in three Messianic persons. It will be remembered that when Jesus wanted to prove the belief in resurrection from the Scriptures, he did not appeal to the book of Daniel (where it appears most clearly) but to the Pentateuch (Ex. 3.6; cf. Matt. 22.32). The regular occurrence of certain series of quotations had suggested to scholars that the writers of the New Testament had similar collections of *testimonia* at their disposal: the similarity between 4Q *Testimonia* and such hypothetical collections is immediately apparent, but we should note a difference in purpose between the Essene and Christian document. The Christian collections, at least in later times, were used for polemic against the Jews, to prove that the messianic promises had been fulfilled; the Essene document was for their own consolation, to reassure themselves, from the presence of the signs of the End, that the Messianic Age is at hand. The same consolatory purpose is probably to be seen in a partially published collection of messianic texts with their appropriate *pešārîm* from the fourth Cave.[2]

Although in these documents the outlines of Essene messianic belief seem homogeneous and clear, the same cannot be said of the *Damascus Document*. Here we are confronted with a disconcerting use of several of the messianic titles. In XIV. 19, 'the Messiah of Aaron and of Israel', the singular, instead of the plural which we found in 1Q S IX. 11, occurs even in the oldest exemplar (75–50 B.C.) of the document from the fourth Cave, 4Q D^b.[3] Here

[1] Cf. 1Q H III. 1–18.

[2] 4Q *Florilegium*, cf. J. M. Allegro, *JBL* LXXV, 1956, pp. 176 f.

[3] The new evidence from Cave IV makes unacceptable my suggestion (see also K. G. Kuhn in K. Stendhal, *The Scrolls and the New Testament*, p. 59) that the Cairo reading is a late medieval correction.

then, certainly, the priestly Messiah has taken over the title of the Kingly one in XIV. 19, but another passage, VII. 18 ff., shows that the old dyarchy subsists under new names in that the 'Interpreter of the Law' and the 'Prince of the Whole Congregation' are distinguished. Moreover, VI. 10 ff. presents us with a puzzling expression when it mentions laws in which one is to walk 'until the rising of the Teacher of Righteousness at the end of days'. Although the form of the title here (*yôreh haṣṣedeq*) differs slightly from that used of the founder of the sect (*môreh haṣṣedeq*) one could assume that the author of the Damascus Document believed in the return of the Teacher of Righteousness *redivivus*; but it could equally well be assumed that the Priestly Messiah took over this title, as he took over that of the Messiah of Israel.

To revert to the three eschatological figures, the Prophet seems scarcely to be mentioned elsewhere in the Qumrân texts and little further can be said about his functions and person. Once it becomes clear that the Priestly Messiah's functions include the proclamation of the eschatological law, it is hard to see what the Prophet can be except a precursor of the Messiah, the Elijah *redivivus* of Mal. 3.23 (EVV 4.5). In Qumrân Cave IV, we have some slight evidence for this. An Aramaic text, studied by Starcky, contains a free Aramaic translation of the passage of Malachi in question, 'I shall send Elijah'. Another, to which Strugnell has drawn my attention, speaks of the *hakkohen hammašiaḥ* who performs the atonement rites, explains the commandments and recognizes the true prophet, as Christ recognized John the Baptist. This preoccupation with the legitimacy of the prophetic precursor can be connected with the expression 'legitimate teacher' in CD VI. 11 (*haṣṣedeq* stressing his legitimacy) where the context is clearly eschatological, as in I Macc. 14.41, where we find the prophetic precursor called a true prophet.

The figures of the Messiah of Aaron and of the Messiah of Israel are a little clearer to us. The writer was the first to point out[1] that the reference was to two separate persons and not merely to one individual who played two roles. This is no longer disputed now. The Messiah of Aaron is the High Priest who is to reveal the true meaning of the Scripture and to promulgate the New Law.

---

[1] *Verbum Domini* XXIX, 1951, p. 152; see also Kuhn, *op. cit.* pp. 54 ff.

Authoritative exposition of the Scriptures is the responsibility of the priesthood, and, for this reason, the Priestly Messiah has the title of 'Interpreter of the Law' (*dôreš hattôrah*) in certain Cave IV texts, and acts in association with the 'Shoot of David'.[1] In the *Rule* and contemporary texts the more important functions of the Priestly Messiah are cultic, but from the *Damascus Document* and into the period when the *pešārîm* are written (first century A.D.) this interpretative function grows in importance. It is only natural that the Essenes expected the Messiah to be born in their circles. This perhaps explains the puzzling expression of CD VII. 18 ff.: 'the Interpreter of the Law who is coming to the land of Damascus'. This cannot be an allusion to the life of the founder of the sect nor to the exodus to Damascus, as the participle *habba'* in itself is atemporal and in this context (with the immediate reference to the Messianic 'Prince of the Whole Congregation') must refer to the future.[2]

The 'Messiah of Israel' corresponds to the traditional 'Messiah of Judah' promised to come forth from the royal Davidic line: for in some texts from Cave IV he is called 'Shoot of David' (cf. Jer. 23.5; 33.15; Zech. 3.8; 6.12).[3] His rôle, however, is confined to political leadership.

In this way the Essenes hoped for a recurrence in the end of days of the situation of the pre-exilic period. They imagined that the kingdom's prosperity was due to the combination of two leaders' authority, one being religious (the High Priest's), the other being temporal (the King's). However, with historical inaccuracy, they ascribed first place to the High Priest and not to the King and projected the theocratic organization of Judaea in the Persian and Hellenistic periods into the future. This detail also fits in well with the priestly origins of the Essene movement, at least in its earlier phase; in the stage represented by the *Commentaries* and the *War* the historical situation brings the messianic king, of Davidic origin, into greater prominence.

It is clear that such a conception of the Messiah is unlike those of the Old and New Testaments, where in the main only the

[1] *JBL* LXXV, 1956, p. 176.
[2] The same connexion between the 'Land of Damascus' and the 'Interpreter of the Law' is to be found also in CD VI. 5, 7.
[3] *JBL* LXXV, 1956, pp. 174-7.

Messiah of royal descent is known.[1] Is there not, however, a trace of this doctrine in the beginning of St Luke's Gospel, where Jesus is 'son of David' by reason of Joseph's family origins (1.32; 3.23–31), but also son of Aaron because Mary his Mother is kinswoman to Elizabeth (1.36), one of the 'daughters of Aaron' (1.5)?

Of the two main functions of the Priestly Messiah in Essene literature, the Gospels developed only that of laying down the messianic Law; Christ's teaching was not merely lay and non-eschatological, like that of the Rabbis, but it had 'authority'. His authority was higher even than that of Moses; in the Sermon on the Mount, after repeating what God had said to Moses, he could say, 'But *I* say unto you . . .' The Johannine maywritings give some importance to the Priestly Messiah, and his cultic functions (not clear in the Synoptic Gospels) are stressed in the Epistle to the Hebrews; the Alexandrian origin of the type of thought found there seems certain, but Essene influence (especially of the Therapeutic type) on the developing thought of the Early Church cannot be excluded from this Epistle.

This brief outline of Essene doctrine shows that it is a link between the Old Testament and the New. But it does not represent a unilinear development from Old Testament teaching; new foreign influences must be allowed to have played their part. Nor can it be denied that the New Testament contains some startling parallels to the teaching of the Essene texts; but it is by being integrated into the 'Christ-event' (the 'Christusgeschehen' of the German exegetes) that these elements are changed, and that the Christian Messiah attains a stature and importance far greater than that of the Essene Messiahs, and does a work that no Essene Messiah would have been able or expected to do.

---

[1] Cf., however, for the OT Zech. 4.14, Jer. 33.14–18; for the NT, cf. O. Cullmann, *Die Christologie des NT* (Tübingen 1957), pp. 82 ff. and esp. pp. 104 ff. On the Synoptics, contrast G. Friedrich, 'Beobachtungen zur messianischen Hohepriesterwartung in den Synoptikern', *Zeitschrift für Theologie und Kirche* LIII, pp. 265 ff.

V

THE DISCOVERIES IN THE JUDAEAN
WILDERNESS AND THEIR IMPORTANCE

OUR discussion of the discoveries in the Judaean Wilderness has concentrated mainly on the Qumrân manuscripts and settlement. It is, however, worth our while to consider the manuscripts that have been recovered as a whole and to draw up a balance sheet of them, so as to bring out more clearly their historical importance.

DOCUMENTS SPREAD OVER TWO THOUSAND YEARS

As far as ancient manuscripts were concerned, Palestine had produced before 1947 only the group discovered at 'Auja Ḥafir, the ancient Nessana, in the Negeb (1935–7). This was a collection of Greek and Arabic papyri from the late Byzantine period and from the beginning of the Arab period in Palestine. Now the discoveries made over the last ten years in the Wilderness of Judaea have given us manuscripts ranging from the eighth century B.C. to the tenth century A.D.

Earliest of all is a palimpsest papyrus from Murabba'ât. Its first text can be recognized as a letter, but it has been so assiduously washed off that decipherment is practically impossible. On top of this a list of four personal names with symbols and figures can be made out; its language is Hebrew, its script Phoenician. This document dates to the eighth century B.C., and no older Semitic papyrus is known. Only Egypt hieroglyphic and hieratic papyri antedate it.

Mention should also be made of two inscribed sherds from Murabba'ât, which should be dated palaeographically to the end of the second century B.C. One of them has only a few letters, but the other bears a text in a fairly archaic type of Aramaic. Though fragmentary, it is eleven lines long.

There is an Aramaic contract from Murabba'ât which is dated to the second year of Nero (A.D. 56), but most of the texts from this site and from another cave which has not yet been located belong to the Second Jewish Revolt (A.D. 132–5) and the immediately preceding decades. These texts are either biblical or else non-literary (i.e. contracts, letters, lists of personal names, etc., plates 18, 22–25). A few Greek and Latin documents come from the military outpost that was established at Murabba'ât after the Revolt.

Lastly, Ḥirbet Mird has produced a series of texts dating from the fifth to the eighth centuries A.D., and Murabba 'ât a few fragments in Arabic, written on cotton paper, which are as late as the tenth century.

THE LINGUISTIC IMPORTANCE OF THE DISCOVERIES

Eight languages are represented in the texts from the Judaean Desert; biblical Hebrew, Mishnaic Hebrew, Palestinian Aramaic, Nabatean, Greek, Latin, Christian Palestinian Aramaic, and Arabic.

The documents from Qumrân are mainly written in *neo-classical Hebrew*, i.e. an imitation at a later date of the language and style of the books of the Bible. As is to be expected in such a case, the result is a language lacking in spontaneity and, in addition, contaminated by the contemporary colloquial dialect. This movement of a return to classical Hebrew fits in well with the general Jewish renaissance which started in Maccabean times.

The copper rolls from Cave III have preserved for us the oldest known text to be written in *Mishnaic Hebrew*; palaeographically, it is to be dated to the middle of the first century A.D. The same language is used in some contracts and all the letters from the Second Revolt. Further, there are two works found in several copies in Cave IV, which antedate the copper rolls, and which are written in a neo-classical Hebrew with features, however, proper to the Mishnaic dialect (such as the frequent use of the participle instead of the indicative and of the relative *š* instead of *'ašer*). This literary Mishnaic dialect reminds one strongly of Qohelet. So from both the third and first centuries B.C. we now have examples of the attempt to use the spoken dialect for literary purposes. The copper rolls and the documents from the Second Revolt prove beyond reasonable doubt that Mishnaic was the normal language of the Judaean population in the Roman period.

Some Jewish scholars (e.g. Segal, Klausner) had already suggested this on the basis of Talmudic anecdotes; additional evidence can be found in the inscriptions on contemporary ossuaries. The presence of Hebrew, besides Greek and Aramaic, on the ossuaries (which represent the use of the middle classes) surely attests that this was a natural language in that milieu and not merely a religious use of the classical Holy Tongue. For instance, the Bethphage lid, the pay-list of an undertaker's employees, is in Hebrew. After A.D. 135 and the almost complete depopulation of Judaea, Hebrew ceased to be used as a colloquial language, although it was preserved in rabbinic circles. Its use, however, may have continued in the Jewish settlements of southern Palestine (*Daroma*), as is evidenced by some papyri of the Byzantine period, which were found in Egypt, but addressed to the Gaza region.[1]

We can then pose the problem of the origins of Mishnaic in new terms. Since there are striking points of contact between the Punic of Roman Africa and the Mishnaic Hebrew of Judaea, it is perhaps reasonable to consider both languages as descendants of a *koine*, which developed at the beginning of the Persian period out of Hebrew as it was spoken in Judaea and Phoenician as spoken on the coast of Palestine. An allusion to such a development may be found in a passage in Nehemiah's memoirs (13.24), where the reformer complains that the children of mixed marriages speak a language that is half-Ashdodite and no longer understand the tongue of their fathers.[2]

The Aramaic section of the Book of Daniel was hitherto our only example of literary Aramaic as it was used in Palestine during the Greco-Roman period. It is a direct continuation of *Imperial Aramaic,* a dialect which can be observed in use in international relations from the Assyrian period onwards, but which flourished especially during the period of the Persian Empire. The Aramaic letters in the Book of Ezra are written in it. Numerous

[1] Cf. a Mishnaic letter of the Byzantine period, written from Egypt (?) to a place in the south of Palestine published by A. Cowley, *JQR* XVI, 1903–4, pp. 4–7; also S. Klein, in *Trade, Industry and Crafts in Ancient Palestine (Library of Palestinology of the Jewish Palestine Exploration Society,* IX–X), Jerusalem, 1937, pp. 75–81. Although this letter witnesses to the non-literary use of Mishnaic, this may still be confined to rabbinic circles, as the addressee is a Rabbi and the writer his pupil.

[2] In that period, Ashdodite meant Phoenician, as Ashdod was the Persian administrative capital for the Palestinian sea-coast.

fragments from Cave IV and the Genesis Apocryphon from Cave I can now be added to the Aramaic part of Daniel, and enrich considerably our knowledge of the grammar and vocabulary of the earliest phases of *Palestinian Aramaic*. These texts are partially contemporary with the oral and written catechesis of the apostolic period and they are unique of their kind; the rather complicated problem of the Aramaic substratum of certain parts of the New Testament will be put in a new light by them.

At Murrabba'ât and at the other site which has not yet been located, we find a slightly more developed form of Aramaic; the development is, however, more orthographic than properly linguistic. These documents date from the first third of the second century A.D. and it is well known that, after this time, *Palestinian Aramaic* became differentiated according to region and religious confession. In the Byzantine period, these new dialects became literary languages: in Judaea there were *Jewish Palestinian* (in which the Jerusalem Talmud and Palestinian Targumim are written) and *Christian Palestinian*; farther north, the Samaritan sect used *Samaritan* and in Galilee there was a *Galilean* branch, which is found especially in *Berešit Rabba*, the Rabbinic commentary on Genesis. Only *Christian Palestinian Aramaic* is represented among the texts discovered in the Judaean Desert. Excavations at Ḥirbet Mird produced some parchment fragments and palimpsests of the Bible in that language and a few non-literary texts. One of the latter is a complete letter on papyrus, written by a monk called Gabriel to the superior of the Monastery of Marda -Castellion. There are other known manuscripts written in Christian Palestinian Aramaic, preserved in the monastery of St Catherine in Sinai and in the Omayyad Mosque of Damascus; but the find at Ḥirbet Mird is of special importance, as it gives us for the first time literary texts found in Palestine itself, and non-literary texts composed in that language.

Aramaic was also spoken in the Greco-Roman period in Transjordan. It was the language of the Nabatean kingdom, and it survives in inscriptions scattered widely from the region of Damascus to the South of Palestine and Arabia, from Miletus, Cos, Puteoli and Rome. While in grammar it scarcely differs from Palestinian Aramaic, it has a most characteristic script. At the not yet located site in the Judaean Desert several *Nabataean* papyri were found, and these are of much greater interest than most of the Nabataean inscriptions which consist chiefly of stereotyped funerary and dedicatory formulae. A long contract, published by J. Starcky, deals with the redemption of a property that had been auctioned by its heir, and is noteworthy for its use of legal terminology that is often identical with that of the Talmud (Plate 24).[1] According to the text, the property in question was situated at Maḥôz ʿAglatên—a place not yet identified with any certainty.[2]

PALAEOGRAPHY

Another discipline which will greatly profit by the discoveries made in the Judaean Desert is Palaeography. In the following paragraphs we shall consider only the texts in 'square' and Phoenician scripts from Qumrân and the two sites of the Second Jewish Revolt. At Qumrân, four scripts can be distinguished: the palaeo-Hebrew (or Phoenician) (Plate 5), the 'square' letter of Hebrew book-hand, the cursive, and a mixed script where book-hand forms are mixed with cursives.[3]

When the first fragments in the palaeo-Hebrew script from Cave I were found, it was thought that they should be dated to the fifth or fourth centuries B.C., because the script was fairly similar to that of the Lakiš ostraca and of other pre-exilic inscribed texts. Soon, however, manuscripts were published where some words written in palaeo-Hebrew letters occurred in the

[1]*RB* LXI, 1954, pp. 161–81. Cf. J. J. Rabinowitz, *BASOR* 139, Oct. 1955, pp. 11–14.

[2]Many documents from the time of the Second Jewish Revolt seem to have been carried off by people fleeing before the Roman advance in the Shephelah and the coastal regions. If the same is true of this Nabataean contract, Maḥôz ʿAglatên could be connected with Bethagla. This town is south of Gaza, which stayed under Nabataean political control until the annexation of Nabataea in A.D. 106, and probably remained under its cultural influence much longer. *Maḥoz* would, then, have the meaning of 'port' or 'emporium'; for Bethagla itself was at some distance from the shore. The dual *ʿAglatên* would allude to the twin towns; for other towns separated from their ports in the same area, we should recall Ašdod and Maḥûz ʿAšdod, Jamnia and Maḥûza de Yamnia and, with another word meaning for port, *Mayuma* of Gaza and *Mayuma* of Ascalon: cf. M. Avi-Yonah, Map of Roman Palestine, in *Quarterly of the Department of Antiquities in Palestine* V, 1939, pp. 155–7, 165. For a less plausible identification of Maḥôz ʿAglatên with a similar-sounding site in Transjordan, see J. Starcky, *RB* LXIII, 1956, p. 274, n. 6.

[3]In addition, two cryptic alphabets were found, cf. p. 115.

body of a text written in the book-hand. It therefore became certain that the two types had been used contemporaneously. At the time of the Maccabean 'Renaissance' the old Phoenician script was resuscitated in almost the same form that it had attained in the seventh century in the Kingdom of Judah. It was used for copies of the Scriptures, especially the Pentateuch, and for legends on coins. The archaizing quality of this revival can be seen in the neglect of the later developments in the script which occurred in the Persian period. It is further possible that this revival even antedates the Maccabees, as there is some slight evidence for a literary renaissance in the third century, not only in Judaea, but also in Phoenicia, under the favourable conditions of Ptolemaic rule in Palestine.

The shape of the letters scarcely changes until the start of our era; afterwards, in the first two centuries A.D., a rapid development occurred. Under the influence of written Greek, there was especially a tendency to reduce the various letters all to the same dimension. There are already a few traces of this development in the Qumrân texts, but it is more noticeable on the coins of the First Revolt and reaches its last phase on those of the Second Revolt. After this date, the archaizing script ceased to be used by the Jews: however, among the Samaritans it continues in use even today. The form that it had reached by the first or second century A.D. was adopted and 'canonized' by them for use in the copies they made of the Pentateuch.

Although the epigraphic evidence was very limited, W. F. Albright was able to sketch the outlines of the evolution of the square script as early as 1937.[1] One of his pupils, F. M. Cross, set himself to bring greater detail into this schema after the rich material of Caves I and IV had been discovered, and devoted special attention to the oldest manuscripts from Qumrân.[2] He was able to prove by his analysis that this script was derived from the Aramaic cursive of the Persian and Hellenistic periods. The square script attained its typical form in the second century B.C., i.e. at the time when other regional scripts also, like those of the Nabataeans and Palmyrenes, were beginning to develop towards what would be their typical form.

[1] *JBL* LVI, 1937, pp. 145–76.
[2] *JBL* LXXIV, 1955, pp. 147–71.

Four phases can be distinguished in the evolution of the square script at Qumrân. In the *archaic* phase, it is close to the script of the contemporary Aramaic documents from Egypt, and can be dated to the end of the third century and the first half of the second century B.C. It is only found in a few manuscripts from Cave IV, in particular, a copy of Samuel (Plate 19), one of Exodus and one of Jeremiah. The *Hasmonean* phase of the square script lasts through the second half of the second century and the first half of the first century B.C. This is the really formative period, although in it the scribe still enjoys a large measure of freedom (Plates 7–9, 15, 21). Then comes the *Herodian* phase in which the letters attain a uniform size and a constant shape; in the hands of good scribes this script almost approaches the uniformity of printing (Plates 16, 17 and 20). A few inscriptions of this period present the same script. It may be suggested that in the Herodian period this form was the 'official' script and was also used widely in public life. The Herodian script was replaced, towards the first half of the first century A.D., by what may be called the *ornamental* script. Here the uniformity of size and shape is even more pronounced than in the Herodian: even the final letters are reduced to a size scarcely bigger than that of the rest. Instead of the sober lines of the Herodian letters, florid curves and titles appear everywhere. It was this latter type, slightly developed, which the Rabbis at the Synod of Jamnia chose for use in copying the Scriptures. It is well attested in the biblical manuscripts from Murabba'ât (Plate 18) as well as by some non-literary documents.

Parallel to the calligraphic or 'book' hand, used for copying books and for more or less official inscriptions, there was a cursive script which seems to have evolved, independently of the book hand, from the same Aramaic cursive, and this was used especially in legal documents (Plate 25). It assumed its fully developed form in the first century of our era and is characterized by a tendency to write groups of letters and even whole words with a single movement of the hand; it suppresses those features of any letter which are not indispensable for distinguishing it from others. This type of script is rather rare at Qumrân, but at Murabba'ât it is the dominant script of private documents. After the Second Revolt, however, it fell out of use.

The *mixed* scripts form a special category. They cannot be

dismissed as the result of a scribe's confused and haphazard use of cursive forms in an otherwise 'calligraphic' document. For some letters are in the book hand, while a small group (e.g., the rounded *mem*, looped *tau* and two-stroke *he*), have *consistently* the cursive form. In the fourth cave there are manuscripts in this script from 100 B.C. onwards, and it is also the most commonly used script on the ossuaries. It should therefore be regarded as a special type of script.

HISTORICAL AND ONOMASTIC IMPORTANCE OF THE TEXTS

An outline will now be given of the historical significance of the texts found at the other sites in the Judaean Desert. What has to be said about those from Qumrân itself has already been stated in chapter III, where we discussed the history of the Essenes.

The texts from Murabba'ât provide us with several precise details about the Second Jewish Revolt. Hitherto, we have had to rely on sparse allusions in the classical historians and the Talmud, a few inscriptions and coins. Though the discoveries in the Judaean Desert do not help us to know more exactly the course of the principal events of the war, they do show us how the rebels organized the civil and military government of the country and what motives inspired them.[1]

The leader of the Revolt, Bar Kokhba, or rather, as the new texts call him, Ben Koseba, comes out of the legendary haze with which the Talmud has surrounded him. The historian can now handle two letters sent by him—one of them was perhaps written with his own hand, as there is a resemblance between the script in which the text is written and that of the signature. There is also a letter sent to him, and a reference to his headquarters in a legal contract. The letter signed by him runs as follows (Plate 23):

> Simon, son of Koseba, to Joshua, son of Galgula, and to the men of Kephar Habbarûk, greetings. I take Heaven as witness against me, (that) if anyone of the Galilaeans who are among you should be ill-treated, I will put fetters on your feet as I did to Ben-Aphlul. Simon, son of Koseba . . .[2]

[1] See Additional Note 6.

[2] Cf. *RB* LX, 1953, pp. 276–94 and pl. XIV, and see also H. L. Ginsberg, *BASOR* 131, Oct. 1953, p. 25; Yeivin, *'Atiqot* I, pp. 95–108; S. Birnbaum, *PEQ*, 1954, pp. 23–32.

The term 'Galilaeans' seems to refer to Jewish refugees from Galilee rather than to the Christians who, according to St Justin and Eusebius of Caesarea, were persecuted by Bar Kokhba. The ill-treatment that they suffered can be easily explained on the assumption that, as the food shortage (of which other documents inform us) grew greater, non-Judaeans received a biased treatment.

The contribution that the texts from Ḥirbet Mird can make to our historical knowledge seems to be limited, but in a few details they improve our knowledge of monastic life in Judaea.

The documents from the Second Revolt have also greatly increased our knowledge of toponymy in the Romano-Byzantine period. For example, a contract from Murabba‘ât mentions the village of Ḥnblṭ'. This is probably to be identified with the *Anablata* which, according to a letter of St Epiphanius, lies on the road from Jerusalem to Bethel, and is therefore the present-day Bir Nabâlah, about five miles to the NNW of Jerusalem. Again, in a fragmentary marriage contract from Murabba‘ât there is a mention of a village called Ḥrdwn', where some member of the priestly family of Elyašib was living. In the uncertain manuscript transmission of the Talmud we sometimes find Bet Ḥarôdôn as the place to which the scapegoat was led; the name seems to have survived in Ḥirbet Ḥaredân, a hill in the Judaean Wilderness some three miles from Jerusalem.

LEGAL IMPORTANCE OF THE TEXTS

From the legal point of view it is the contracts from Murabba‘ât and the similar unidentified site which give us the most striking information. They are the first discoveries of the kind made in Palestine, and four languages are represented in them: Mishnaic Hebrew, Palestinian Aramaic, Nabataean and Greek. Through them we have direct contact with the legal institutions and customs of the Roman period and their appropriate formulae, matters which hitherto we had to deduce indirectly from rabbinic texts (and these are more concerned with Jewish jurisprudence, and that of a slightly later perod). At the present early stage in the study of these documents it is becoming apparent that there are points of contact with the forms we find in Babylonian contracts, Aramaic contracts from Elephantine and Greek papyri in Egypt as well as with later Talmudic legal practice.

Here is an example of this material; a deed of sale, written in Aramaic and drawn up towards the end of the Second Jewish Revolt (Plate 25).[1]

> On the twentieth of Adar(?) in the third year of the liberation of Israel in Kephar Bebayu, Ḥadar(?), son of Judah of Kephar Bebayu, said to Eleazar, son of Eleazar, the administrative officer of the same place:
>
> I, of my own free will, today, have sold to you today, a house of mine which on its north opens on to my courtyard, so that you can make an opening for it into your (former) house. But you will have no claim upon me inside that courtyard. I have sold you (that house) for a sum amounting to eight denarii, equal to two tetradrachms. (I have received this amount as) complete payment. Henceforth Eleazar has rights over this house which he has purchased: stones and beams and stairs(?), (and) all that is in it, building and land.
>
> The boundaries of this house [*which belong to you El*] eazar the buyer are: on the east side Jonathan, [*son of Josh*]ua; on the north the courtyard; on the west and south built-up land. You will have no claim upon me inside this courtyard and no right of passage against my, Ḥadar's(?), will from today henceforth. And I am a guarantor and surety for this house you have bought from today onwards.
>
> And I Salome, daughter of Simon, wife of the above mentioned Ḥadar(?), I (*Sa*)lome will have no rights over this house from today onwards. (In case of legal action), damages will be paid to you from the goods we now have and those we may acquire.
>
> This deed is 'plain' and hereto the following have signed:
> Ḥadar(?), son of Judah, on his own behalf.
> Salome, daughter of Simon, has written on her own behalf.
> Eleazar, son of Mattatha, scribe.
> Simon, son of Joseph, witness.
> Eleazar(?), son of . . ., witness.
> Judah, son of Judah, witness.

[1]See J. T. Milik, *Biblica* XXXVIII, 1957, pp. 264 ff. for references to earlier discussions of this document.

THE QUMRÂN TEXTS AND HEBREW LITERATURE

The science which has gained most ground from the discoveries in the Judaean Desert is that of the history of Jewish literature. In this section we will be dealing with Qumrân texts, from Murabba-'ât and Hirbet Mird have produced scarcely any literary works other than copies of books of the Bible.

Before these discoveries, our knowledge of Hebrew literature in the Greco-Roman period was exceedingly sparse. Almost all the works that the Rabbis at Jamnia had left out of the Canon were gradually forgotten. A few books were saved by finding a place in the Alexandrian Canon, the Old Testament of the Christians, e.g. Tobit, Ecclesiasticus, Judith, Maccabees. Some of these books (e.g., II Maccabees, probably the story of Susanna, and perhaps Judith) are original Greek compositions of the Alexandrian Diaspora. But from the great mass of pseudepigraphical and apocalyptic works produced at that time, only a few remained available to us before the Qumrân discoveries, e.g., the Book of Jubilees, those parts of the Book of Enoch which were taken up into a later compilation of Christian origin, résumés of *Testaments* ascribed to some of the Patriarchs, and a few other pseudepigraphical works. One can add to these only some sayings attributed to Rabbis of the Greco-Roman period, the authenticity of which cannot be checked, and a few quotations in the Talmud from books like Ben Sira which were non-canonical in the eyes of Rabbinic Judaism.

The discovery of the Qumrân library fills up this gap in a fairly substantial way; it provides us not only with strictly Essene writings, but also with a selection of other books that they copied, works composed before and during the time of the community's occupation of Qumrân. The works that were written before the community came to Qumrân were mainly pseudepigraphical (with themes especially of priestly interest and usually in Aramaic), liturgical and sapiential. Some works, such as Tobit, the *Description of the New Jerusalem* and an astrological book, survive in both Hebrew and Aramaic copies. This can be explained, if we consider it as a part of the literary and nationalist renaissance which was mentioned above; works that had earlier been composed in Aramaic were later translated into Hebrew. The opposite, 'democratic', tendency of translating the sacred books into Aramaic is less often found at Qumrân. The milieu was too highly cultured for this to be necessary—a strong contrast to the popular and Aramaic-speaking environment of the early Church.

THE DISCOVERIES IN THE JUDAEAN DESERT AND THE HISTORY OF RELIGIONS

The importance of these discoveries for the religious history of the Jewish people cannot be overestimated. Indeed, this aspect of their significance has gained for them a notoriety that spreads far beyond scholarly circles.

The Essene movement, because of its points of contact with Christianity, obviously holds first place in the eyes of the wider circles who are interested in these discoveries. Yet the texts from Murabba'ât are of great interest also, for the picture that they give us of orthodox Judaism in the form that it was beginning to attain between the two Revolts. The biblical fragments found there are a proof of the respect with which the Scriptures were treated. The consonantal text was established in minute detail and copied from a master-scroll, and even today rabbinic Bibles preserve for us the memory of this scroll's corrected mistakes. The 'ornamental' script was regularly employed in the Murabba'ât texts to the exclusion especially of the palaeo-Hebrew. Detailed rules concerning the copying of the sacred books and the manner in which they should be set out on the sheets of leather were observed. Not until later in the Byzantine period were these rules written down in the Talmudic tractate *Sopherim* ('Scribes'), but we can now see that the *textus receptus* and the prescriptions concerning its transmission had already attained their final form between the two Revolts. A great contrast becomes apparent, when one compares this situation with that of the former period as shown in the Qumrân library, where we can see the great freedom exercised in choosing between various recensions and orthographic or calligraphic conventions.

The Second Revolt presents us, therefore, with a strictly orthodox milieu. Hardly anything was read in it except the books of the Palestinian Canon. Even the choice of passages to be written in phylacteries had now become fixed, whereas in the days of the Essenes great variation prevailed (Plate 22). The Sabbath was scrupulously observed, as is shown by a letter which requests the addressee to give lodging to a special envoy so that he can observe the Sabbath rest. The same messianic hope that had inspired the Essenes was still very much alive; indeed, this was the dominant factor in the Second Revolt. For the rebels and the masses believed that the restoration of the Kingdom of Israel, with its *two* Messiahs, the King and the High Priest, was about to come to pass. The military leader of the Revolt, Simon Ben Koseba, was hailed as 'Star of Jacob' and 'Prince of Israel', titles used of the Messiah also at Qumrân. The title of 'Prince of Israel', stamped on the dictator's coins, is also found in the Murabba'ât texts.[1] While the 'Son of the Star' (Bar Kokhba) was represented as the Messiah of Israel, the role of the priestly Messiah of Aaron seems to have fallen upon the obscure figure of 'Eleazar, the (High) Priest', who likewise appears on the coins of the Revolt.

This fervour of Messianic hope and the intense disillusionment that followed upon the failure of the Revolt are well reflected in a dialogue set on the lips of two famous Rabbis. 'When Rabbi 'Aqiba saw Bar Kozeba, he quoted (the biblical verse), "A star is risen from Jacob". And he commented on it, saying, "Kozeba is risen from Jacob and it is he who is the King-Messiah". Rabbi Joḥanan Ben Ṭorta replied, "Grass will grow between your jaws, but the Son of David will still not have come".'[2]

As for the writings of the Essenes, they have a double importance for the history of the Jewish religion. They have a place both in the line of development which leads to the writings of the New Testament and in that which finishes in Pharisaic Judaism, as the Mishnah and Talmud depict it. Furthermore, as we have seen, they form in themselves an essentially authentic development from the Old Testament. Their theology is centred in eschatology, it is true, but this is already becoming strong in the later books of the Old Testament. Their piety gives a large place to personal religious life and aspires to an intimate union with God and his angels.

[1] The messianic significance of 'Prince of Israel' does not exclude a certain normal military meaning as well, as appears from a phrase in one of the Murabba'ât texts 'Prince of Israel in the field'.

[2] *Echa Rabba*, II. 2, cf. *RB* LX, 1935, pp. 289–92.

The multitude of legal prescriptions which controlled the rhythm of the Essene's daily life should not make one forget the other elements which played their part in forming this type of spiritual outlook. It is, however, this legal aspect which becomes dominant among the Pharisees, to such an extent that they tended to set man's relations with God almost exclusively on the level of legal observances.

The relations between Essenism and early Christianity can be considered under three heads: we find literary, institutional, and doctrinal similarities. Between the Synoptic Gospels and the Qumrân texts there seem to be relatively few literary parallels. Matt. 11.25–27 is an exception to this general rule, but this passage has long been recognized to clash with the usual style of the Synoptics, and has been characterized as a Johannine intrusion. It is notably with John and Paul that the greatest number of points of contact, both literary and doctrinal, have been discovered.[1]

As for institutional parallels, we have already shown in some detail that the organization of the early Church, as it appears in Acts and the Pauline epistles, adopted in a certain way the same organization as the Essene sect had had. So, for instance, in the summary in Acts (2.42–7) of the activities of the first Christians, we find reference made to 'community of property', 'prayer' and 'teaching'. Likewise, the Essene sacred meal has to be closely connected with what we learn from Paul and the *Didache* about the ordinances for liturgical gatherings (the *eucharistia* and the *agapê*).

One has the impression that there is a perpetual increase in Essene influence on the early Church. In the generation of our Lord and of his first disciples there are hardly any similarities. In the earliest phase of the Church in Palestine, as we find it in Acts, institutional parallels become more frequent. Slightly later we find in one part of the Church Essene influence almost taking over and submerging the authentically Christian doctrinal ele-

[1]See the work of F. Notscher, *Zur Theologischen Terminologie der Qumrân-Texte* (Bonner Biblische Beiträge 10) Bonn 1956; R. E. Murphy, 'The Dead Sea Scrolls and New Testament Comparisons', *Catholic Biblical Quarterly* XVIII, 1956, pp. 263 ff.; and the essays collected in the volume *The Scrolls and the New Testament* edited by K. Stendahl.

ment; indeed, it may be considered responsible for the break between the Judaeo-Christians and the Great Church.

However, there are numerous similarities between Essene and the authentic early Christian doctrine. Both hold the eschatological concept of the true Israel ruled by twelve leaders; both believe that they have already in this life a foretaste of the blessedness that the end of days will bring about; both believe that the spirits of good and evil are engaged in struggle both in the cosmos and in the soul of each man, and in both systems, the believer shares already in the life of the angels. In early Christianity, however, all these features, and many others too, are taken up into a new doctrinal structure and the integration of these elements with the central beliefs of the new faith transforms each one of them. Sometimes the transformation is merely qualitative, certain elements being more stressed and assuming a greater importance in the new system. For instance, both groups believe that the call to salvation is addressed to all men, without ethnic or social limitations, and that men are brothers, and God a Father to every man; both Communities of the Elect live in an atmosphere impregnated with forgiveness and love. But in other cases the adoption of Essene beliefs into an organic unity with the new doctrines completely transforms them. So, for instance, the period of the End has for the Christian already been inaugurated with the coming of the Messiah. Further, the sense of the sinfulness of human nature is so radicalized that a merely human mediation of the New Covenant and a merely human Messiah would no longer seem effective. God must become Man and make the covenant by atoning himself for our sins. God meets man in the intimacy of his being, and this meeting bears its fruits in a 'rebirth' where a 'new creature' is 'born from on high'.

Accordingly, although Essenism bore in itself more than one element that one way or another fertilized the soil from which Christianity was to spring, it is nevertheless evident that the latter religion represents something completely new which can only be adequately explained by the person of Jesus himself.

CHRONOLOGICAL TABLE

Jewish Political History	*Essene History*[1]
175–64 *Antiochus IV Epiphanes*	Mention of *'ntykws* (QT)
167 Jewish Revolt, raised by Mattathias and his sons, helped by the Asidaeans (*Hasidim*).	
166–60 Judas Maccabaeus	
162–50 *Demetrius I Soter*	
160–42 Jonathan	
152 Alexander Balas lands at Ptolemais (Acre) Johathan starts to rebuild Jerusalem Jonathan named High Priest by Alexander	
150–45 *Alexander Balas*	*c.* 150 Exodus of Essenes to Qumrân, led by the Teacher of Righteousness (QT) Modest building operations at Q (Phase Ia)
150–49 Jonathan named military and civil governor of Judaea by Alexander	*c.* 150–43 Persecution of Essenes by Wicked priest; his visit to Qumrân (QT) *c.* 146 First mention of Essenes in Jos.
145–38 *Demetrius II*	
145–2 *Antiochus VI*	
c. 145 Jonathan named governor of Syria by Antiochus VI	
144–2 Rebuilding of Jerusalem	Wicked Priest rebuilds 'City of Vanity' (QT)
143 Tryphon imprisons Jonathan 142 and executes him	Capture and death of Wicked Priest (QT)

[1] In brackets, we give our evidence. QT = Qumrân Texts, Q Exc. = Excavations, Jos. = Josephus.

143–34 Simon appointed by Demetrius High Priest and Ethnarch of the Jews

Two brothers, 'vessels of violence rebuild city (QT)

141 Simon and his sons appointed High Priests for ever, by popular vote

140–38 *Tryphon*

Seleucid silver coins (Q Exc.)

138–29 *Antiochus VII Sidetes*

134–04 John Hyrcanus I, High Priest and Ethnarch.

'False prophet' (QT)

129–5 *Demetrius II (bis)*

Bronze coins of Hyrcanus and his successors (Q Exc.)

? Death of Teacher of Righteousness

c. 110 Hyrcanus persecutes Pharisees

Enlarging of Qumrân buildings (Phase Ib)

Exodus to Land of Damascus (QT)

104–3 Aristobulus I High Priest and King

An Essene predicts his death (Jos.)

103–76 Alexander Jannaeus

95–78 *Demetrius III Eukairos*

95–76 Jannaeus struggles for power with Pharisees

88 [*Dm*]*trys* fails to take Jerusalem (QT) 'Lion of Wrath' crucifies many of his enemies (QT)

Mention of *Šlmṣywn* (QT)

76–67 Alexandra (*Šalamṣiyôn*) Queen, Hyrcanus II High Priest

67 Hyrcanus II King

67–3 Aristobulus II High Priest and King

66–2 *Pompey in the East*

64 *Syria becomes a Roman Province*

'Rising of the rulers of the Kittiim' (QT)

63 Pompey captures Jerusalem

63–40 Hyrcanus II High Priest

62 *Aemilius Scaurus, governor of Syria*

Massacres by '*mlyws* (QT)

47–1 Hyrcanus II appointed Ethnarch

40–37 Antigonus High Priest and King

40–38 *Parthian Invasion*

c. 38 (?) Qumrân settlement burnt (Q Exc.)

40 Hyrcanus II captured and mutilated

37–4 Herod the Great King

                            31 (Jos.) Earthquake damages Qum-
                               rân (Q Exc.)

30 Hyrcanus II strangled   ?–*c.* 4 Gap in occupation of Qumrân
                               (Q Exc.)

                            Herod favours the Essenes (Jos.)

4 Varus' campaign

4 B.C.–A.D. 6 Archelaus Ethnarch of   *c.* 4 Essene reconstruction of Qum-
Judaea and Samaria   rân (Q Exc.) (Phase II)

54–68 *Nero*

66–70 First Jewish Revolt   Some Essenes take part in Revolt
                           (Jos.)

                          68 Summer. Destruction of Qum-
                           rân (Q Exc.)

                          68–end of 1st cent. Roman Fort at
                           Qumrân (Q Exc.)

69–79 *Vespasian*

117–38 *Hadrian*

13205 Revolt under Simon ben   Qumrâm, Murabba'ât, etc., centres
Koseba   of Jewish rebels

BIBLIOGRAPHY

I. Editions

I. Qumran Manuscripts.

(a) Cave I

M. BURROWS, with the assistance of J. C. TREVER and W. H. BROWNLEE, *The Dead Sea Scrolls of St Mark's Monastery*, Vol. I: The Isaiah Manuscript and the Habakkuk Commentary, New Haven, 1950; Vol. II, Fascicle 2: Plates and Transcription of the Manual of Discipline, New Haven 1951.

E. L. SUKENIK (prepared for the press by N. AVIGAD), *'Osar hammegillot haggenuzot šebide ha'universita ha'ibrit*, Jerusalem 1954. English edition: *The Dead Sea Scrolls of the Hebrew University*, Jerusalem 1955.

D. BARTHÉLEMY, O.P., and J. T. MILIK, with contributions by R. DE VAUX, O.P., G. M. CROWFOOT, H. J. PLENDERLEITH, G. L. HARDING, *Qumran Cave I* (Discoveries in the Judaean Desert, I), Oxford 1955.

N. AVIGAD and Y. YADIN, *A Genesis Apocryphon. A Scroll from the Wilderness of Judaea*. Description and contents of the scroll, facsimiles, transcription and translation of columns II, XIX–XXII, Jerusalem 1956 (Hebr. and Eng.).

(b) Cave II

M. BAILLET, 'Fragments araméens de Qumran 2. Description de la Jérusalem Nouvelle', *RB* LXII, 1955, pp. 222–45.

(c) Cave III

J. T. MILIK, *VT* Suppl. IV, 1957, pp. 22 ff., gives extracts from the Copper Rolls.

R. DE VAUX, *RB* LX, 1953, pp. 555 ff. (beginning of a *pešer* on Isaiah).

(d) Cave IV

J. M. ALLEGRO, 'A Newly-discovered Fragment of a Commentary on Psalm XXXVII from Qumran', *PEQ* 1954, pp. 69–75.
'Further light on the History of the Qumran Sect', *JBL* LXXV, 1956, pp. 89–95.
'Further Messianic References in Qumran Literature', *ibid.*, pp. 174–87.

F. M. CROSS, Jr., 'A New Qumran Biblical Fragment related to the Original Hebrew Underlying the Septuagint', *BASOR* 132, December 1953, pp. 15–26.
'A Manuscript of Samuel in an Archaic Jewish Bookhand from Qumran: 4Q Sam*b*', *JBL* LXXIV, 1955, pp. 165–72.

C. H. Huntzinger, 'Fragmente einer älteren Fassung des Buches Milhamā aus Höhle 4 von Qumran', *ZAW* LXIX, 1957, pp. 131–51.

K. G. Kuhn, *Phylakterien aus Höhle 4 von Qumran* (Ahhandlungen der Heidelberger Akademie der Wissenschaften, Philos.-Hist. Klasse, 1957, I) Heidelberg, 1957.

J. T. Milik, 'Le Testament de Lévi en araméen. Fragment de la Grotte IV de Qumran', *RB* LXII, 1955, pp. 398–406.
' "Prière de Nabonide" et autres écrits d'un cycle de Daniel. Fragments araméens de Qumran', *RB* LXIII, 1956, pp. 407–15.
'Deux Documents Inédits du Désert de Juda, I. Psaumes . . .' *Biblica* XXXVIII, 1957, pp. 245–55.
'Hénoch au pays des aromates', *RB* LXV, 1958, pp. 70–77.

J. Muilenburg, 'A. Qobeleth Scroll from Qumrân', *BASOR* 135, October 1954, pp. 20–28.
'Fragments of Another Qumran Isaiah Scroll', *ibid.*, pp. 28–32.

P. W. Skehan, 'A Fragment of the "Song of Moses" (Deut. 32) from Qumran', *BASOR* 136, December, 1954, pp. 12–15.
'Exodus in the Samaritan Recension from Qumran', *JBL* LXXIV, 1955, pp. 182–7.
'The Qumran Manuscripts and Textual Criticism', *VT* Suppl. IV, 1957, pp. 148–160, gives fragments of Greek manuscripts of Leviticus and Numbers.

M. Testuz, 'Deux fragments inédits des manuscripts de la Mer Morte', *Semitica* V, 1955, p. 37 f.

(*e*) Cave VI

M. Baillet, 'Fragments du document de Damas: Qumran, Grotte VI', *RB* LXIII, 1956, pp. 513–23.

(*f*) Cairo Geniza

C. Rabin, *The Zadokite Documents: I. The Admonition. II. The Laws, edited with a Translation and Notes,* Oxford, 1954.

S. Zeitlin, *The Zadokite Fragments* (JQR Monograph Series I), Philadelphia, 1952, gives poor facsimiles.

2. *Murabba'ât Documents.*

J. T. Milik, 'Une lettre de Siméon bar Kokheba', *RB* LX, 1953, pp. 276–94.

R. de Vaux, 'Quelques textes hébreux de Murabba'at', *ibid.*, pp. 268–75.

P. Benoit, *Une reconnaissance de dette du IIème siècle en Palestine,* Scritti in onore di Paribeni e Calderini II, Milano 1957, pp. 257–72.

3. *Unidentified Site* (Second Revolt).

D. Barthélemy, 'Redécouverte d'un chaînon manquant de l'histoire de la Septante', *RB* LX, 1953, pp. 18–29.

Bibliography

J. T. Milik, 'Un contrat juif de l'an 134 après J.-C.,' *RB* LXI, 1954, pp. 182–90.
'Deux documents inédits du Désert de Juda; II. Acte de vente d'un terrain', *Biblica* XXXVIII, 1957, pp. 255–64.

J. Starcky, 'Un contrat nabatéen sur papyrus', *RB* LXI, 1954, pp. 161–81.

4. *Documents from Ḥirbet Mird.*

J. T. Milik, 'Une inscription et une lettre en araméen christo-palestinien', *RB* LX, 1953, pp. 526–39.

II. *Selected books*

J. M. Allegro, *The Dead Sea Scrolls* (Penguin Books), Harmondsworth 1956.

M. Burrows, *The Dead Sea Scrolls,* London 1956.
More Light on the Dead Sea Scrolls, London 1958.

F. M. Cross, Jr., *The Ancient Library of Qumran and Modern Biblical Studies,* New York 1958.

A. Dupont-Sommer, *The Jewish Sect of Qumran and the Essenes. New Studies on the Dead Sea Scrolls,* London 1954 (a revised translation of *Nouveaux Aperçus sur les Manuscrits de Qumran,* Paris 1953).

K. Elliger, *Studien zum Habakuk-Kommentar vom Toten Meer*, Tübingen 1953.

Y. Licht, *The Thanksgiving Scroll* (Hebrew), Jerusalem 1957.

F. Nötscher, *Zur Theologischen Terminologie der Qumran-Texte,* Bonn 1956.

C. Rabin, *Qumran Studies* (Scripta Judaica II), Oxford 1957.

H. H. Rowley, *The Zadokite Fragments and the Dead Sea Scrolls,* Oxford 1952.

K. Stendahl, Ed., *The Scrolls and the New Testament,* London 1958.

G. Vermes, *Discovery in the Judaean Desert,* New York 1956.

Y. Yadin, *The Scroll of the War of the Sons of Light against the Sons of Darkness* (Hebrew), Jerusalem 1955.

III. *Translations of the Non-Biblical Texts*

The editions of Avigad and Yadin (*A Genesis Apocryphon*), and Barthélemy and Milik (*Qumran Cave I*) contain translations of the texts edited by them. Furthermore the books by Burrows and Vermès cited above contain translations of much of the texts. In addition to them:

W. H. Brownlee, *The Dead Sea Manual of Discipline, BASOR* Supplementary Studies 10–12, New Haven 1951.

J. Carmignac, *La Règle de la Guerre des Fils de la Lumière contre les Fils des Ténèbres,* Paris 1958.

A. Dupont-Sommer, 'Le Livre de Hymnes découvert près de la Mer Morte (*IQH*)', *Semitica* VII, 1957 (whole volume).

T. H. Gaster, *The Scriptures of the Dead Sea Sect in English Translation,* London 1957 (sometimes tending to paraphrase).

IV. *Discussions in books and articles*

It is impossible to mention here the hundreds of titles which should fall under this heading. We must content ourselves with reference to other bibliographies.

C. Burchard, *Bibliographie zu den Handschriften vom Toten Meer, ZAW* Beihefte 76, Berlin 1957, gives a *classified* and selective bibliography up to Autumn 1956.

P. Nober, *Elenchus Bibliographicus Biblicus,* in Biblica, covers also the more recent period. Although in some respects more complete, works relevant to Qumrân are scattered over the *Elenchus,* without complete cross references to all the literature.

Internationale Zeitschriftenschau für Bibelwissenschaft und Grenzgebiete is less complete but gives short summaries of the articles cited.

ADDITIONAL NOTES

1, to p. 15. Among the caves found after the survey of 1952 two are especially noteworthy. From a cave in the Wadi Qumrân, found by Ta'âmireh in September 1952, come two jars and five juglets, now in the Palestine Archaeological Museum. One of the jars bears an inscription in charcoal, indicating its capacity—'2 *se'ah* and 7 *log*'. From the volume of the jar, the value of the *se'ah* can be established at *c.* 15.5 litres (3½ gallons). Almost identical values for the *se'ah* have been obtained from pottery of the eighth and seventh centuries B.C. (jars from Lakiš). The conservative tendencies of Jerusalem and the Temple may have been responsible for the maintenance of the official metrological system of the monarchy into the time of the Second Temple.

Another small cave, with a terrace in front of it, was discovered above 'Ain Fešḥa by myself in the spring of 1958. It contained two distinct strata, the lower with Iron II sherds, and the upper with pottery of the Qumrân type mixed with ashes, and, in a corner, a neat pile of date stones; this was probably the kitchen and store cave of an Essene hermit who lived in a hut on the terrace.

2, to pp. 21 and 46. De Vaux has given, in *RB* LXV, 1958, pp. 406–8, an account of his latest season at 'Ain Fešḥa, one and a half miles south of Ḥirbet Qumrân. Excavations uncovered a fairly large structure with two doors facing east; this consists of a courtyard surrounded by storage rooms and living quarters. The evidence of the pottery and coins shows that this building, an agricultural centre, was occupied at the same time as the Ḥirbeh, from the end of the second century B.C until the end of the First Jewish Revolt, with a similar gap towards the end of the first century B.C.; and was reoccupied for a short period during the Second Jewish Revolt. South of this complex there is a large enclosure, with a paved area, perhaps used for drying dates (cf. p. 49). To the north there is a large courtyard containing several tanks connected by canals. On the basis of certain indications de Vaux thinks that this was an installation for the preparing and tanning of leather; he restricts its use to the preparation and tanning of real leather for shoes, straps and tools, not of the untanned skins used for the manuscripts. We consider it, however, probable that the sectarians themselves prepared skins for their manuscripts either at Fesha or at Qumrân, although the instruments required for this work, being less substantial than those discovered by de Vaux, would easily disappear. To buy prepared skins from the outside world would represent a very heavy expenditure for the community, even if it no longer lived in complete economic isolation. We may note that the decline in copying activity in Greek monasteries in the Middle Ages was due in great part to the poverty of the communities who could not afford to buy new parchment.

3, to p. 38. Some results of my further study of the 4Q manuscripts of the *Damascus Document* may be added. On the evidence of two manuscripts, we have now to change the order of pages proposed by Schechter and followed by all subsequent editors of the Cairo manuscript. Pages XV and XVI precede page IX *directly*; these two pages and the beginning of page IX both give laws relating to oaths and vows. After page VIII and the conclusion to the historical section (missing in A, preserved in B, page XX, cf. p. 60), but before page XV, we can detect the loss of several pages in the Cairo manuscript A. Numerous fragments from the Cave IV manuscripts belong to this missing section. These contain prescriptions concerning the cultic purity of priests and sacrifices; a more detailed treatment of the law of diseases (Lev. 13.29 ff.) and an expanded version of Lev. 15 (fluxes of men and women), laws of marriage, prescription relating to agricultural life, the payment of tithes, relations with pagans, relations between the sexes, a prohibition of magic, etc.

To sum up, the original order of the work was as follows: Opening columns (4Q, missing in Cairo manuscript), CD.I–VIII (and a text parallel to *fin.* XIX–XX), missing part (partly preserved in 4Q), XV–XVI, IX–XIV, final columns (4Q: penal code, and liturgy for the feast of the Renewal of the Covenant, cf. pp. 116 f.).

4, to p. 52. The closest parallel to the Qumrân aqueduct is the one that supplies the fortress of Hyrcanion, built by Hyrcanus I and thus contemporary with the Qumrân water installations. I had an occasion recently to study its early sections in the Wadi Ennâr (near the monastery of Mar Saba). It was built on the deep gorge's northern slope so that it would be able to trap all the rainfall. The way in which the channel is cut into and through the rock, and built up on stone fills at places where the rock drops away, so as to maintain the water's level, the dimensions of the aqueduct itself, the composition of the plaster—all these details are identical in the Hyrcania and Qumrân aqueducts.

5, to p. 107. Further study of the *Mišmarôt* from Cave IV, not yet finished, seems to favour the assumption that the Essenes computed the beginning of *their* lunar month from the full moon, not the new moon. Nevertheless, in one of their synchronistic tables, in addition to the correspondence between the day of their solar calendar and the first day of their lunar month they also note the day of the solar month on which the *new* moon falls; this correspondence is called *dauqah* or *duqyah,* which in Rabbinic literature means 'precision (obtained by an observation)' the root *dwq* meaning 'to examine, observe'. There also seems to be no doubt that they reckoned the day as starting with sunrise and not sunset.

6, to p. 136. Further study of the documents from Murabba'ât has enabled me to reconstruct in some greater detail the military and political course of the Second Jewish Revolt. This reconstruction will be published in *Les Grottes de Murabba'ât* (Discoveries in the Judaean Desert, Vol. II, Oxford) which is shortly to appear.

INDEX OF SUBJECTS

INDEX OF PASSAGES CITED

1. Qumrân Cave I. The original entry is high in the rock face; the large entry lower down was made by the clandestine excavators.

2. Jars from Qumrân. This type was used for storing manuscripts.

3. Qumrân Cave IV (with one man standing on top of it and another inside) and Cave V (to its right) in the marl terrace of Qumrân.

4. Qumrân Cave XI. A typical hermit's cave, in the cliff face.

5. Fragments of Exodus in palaeo-Hebrew script, from Qumrân Cave IV.

6. Fragments of the Song of Moses (Deut. 32) from Qumrân Cave IV, translated on p. 24.

7. Fragments of Qohelet (Ecclesiastes) from Qumrân Cave IV, dating from the 2nd century B.C., *c.* 100 years after the book was composed.

8. Opening of the *Prayer of Nabonidus* from Qumrân Cave IV, translated on pp. 36 f.

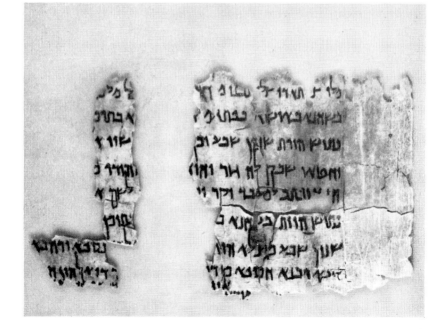

9. The older Isaiah manuscript from Cave I (*c.* 100 B.C.) opened at chapters 40 and 41.

10. The pantry. The writer cleaning the shattered stacks of pottery.

11. Tables from the scriptorium, reconstructed in the Museum at Jerusalem.

12. A cistern split by the earthquake of 31 B.C. The level to the left of the fault is 50 cm. lower.

13. Pottery and coins from Qumrân. In the centre, one of the three caches of silver. The coins were minted in Tyre.

14. The meeting hall at Qumrân, orientated east-west, the assembly facing Jerusalem.

15. The *Rule of the Community* from Cave I, column IX. At line 11 there is the passage about the coming of a Prophet and two Messiahs (cf. p. 124).

16. The *Hodayot* (Hymns) from Cave I, column I.

17. The opening column of the *Rule for the War* from Cave I.

18. Fragment of Exodus from Murabba'ât. The Hebrew book-hand will not develop far beyond this point until the Middle Ages.

19. A fragment of I Samuel, from Cave IV translated on pp. 25 f. This manuscript was written towards the end of the third century B.C. and is the oldest known biblical manuscript. The variation in the size of the letters is a sign of the script's antiquity.

20. Fragment of a manuscript of Isaiah from Cave IV, in the standardized writing of the beginning of our era.

21. The Testimony Document from Qumrân Cave IV, discussed on pp. 61 ff. and 124 f.

22. Part of a complete phylactery from Murabbaʿât. This piece contains the Shemaʿ (Deut. 6.4–9). Enlarged three times.

23. Autograph letter from Simon ben Koseba, leader of the Second Jewish Revolt. Translated on p. 136.

24. The first Nabataean papyrus ever found; a deed concerning the title to some properties, dating from about A.D. 100.

25. A Jewish contract in Aramaic, written in the cursive script. It is dated 'the year 3 of the freedom of Israel'. Translated on p. 128.